PRAISE FOR
THERE WERE NO FLOWERS

"Put a scalpel in the hand of a young A~~meric~~al resident and you have a surg~~e~~ ~~th~~e resident to Vietnam at the l ~~be~~ming surgery in admissions wa ng to the continuous anguished ~~~~ ~~and~~ dying, the resident must now be the surgeon he was destined to become, only years sooner.

"Dr. Meffert, a distinguished cardiovascular surgeon, has written a compelling account of his tending to the traumatic wounds of soldiers on all sides of the conflict.

"As readers, we stand beside him as he finds his way through dealing with severe injuries. We come to realize the intense dedication of men and women who offer care in circumstances of great peril. We are inspired to grow with them into bravery and kind service for others.

"Still another story lies embedded here, one not only of personal sources of determination and resiliency but also of an emotional journey. Father and son travel to Normandy, France, where the eldest of three surgeons once tended wounded soldiers on Omaha Beach during World War II. Dr. Meffert's life and legacy is told with grace and honesty."

—Randall Weingarten, MD, Department of Psychiatry and Behavioral Sciences, Stanford University Medical Center

"Dr. William Meffert made many real-life decisions during his time in Vietnam, which he shares with all of us. This book impacted me personally, as I am a Vietnam vet from 1968, serving in the Ninth Infantry and First Logistical Command.

"I say to Bill as a comrade in arms in Vietnam, 'Thanks for sharing your experiences, and thank you for being there.' I certainly recommend this book to vets and to all adults to learn what actually happens in wars and how physicians who treat cataclysmic injuries of soldiers with minimal preoperative information must frequently make decisions critical to others."

—Frank Rydzewski, former platoon machine gunner; semiretired professor, International Business Department, University of South Carolina

"Medicine is a lens into both the most incredible and the most gruesome aspects of human existence. This is particularly true in the specialty of trauma surgery. It takes courage, patience, and a great respect for fellow human beings to unpack experiences in the field, relive them, and share them with such clarity, vivid detail, and honesty. It is a privilege to be privy to the thoughts and stories of Dr. William Meffert, who rises to this duty and challenge with grit and integrity."

—Arany Uthayakumar, MD candidate, Zucker School of Medicine, Hofstra/Northwell

"Dr. William Meffert's father, Dr. Clyde Meffert, served in Europe during World War II at an evacuation hospital at Omaha Beach, and twenty-eight years later Dr. William

Meffert served at the Ninety-Fifth Evacuation Hospital in Vietnam. The kind of injuries and medical capabilities were quite different between the two conflicts, but the dedication of our doctors, nurses, and medical personnel remained the same.

"Dr. Meffert and I both arrived at the Ninety-Fifth Evacuation Hospital in Da Nang, Vietnam, in the fall of 1968. He had excellent training from Yale University, and I, from the University of Missouri. Like thousands of soldiers' families, our devoted wives and children were without us for the next year.

"In Vietnam, Dr. Meffert's surgical skills and knowledge saved many lives and gave comfort to our brave young soldiers. There were no training programs that adequately prepared physicians and nurses for the numbers and type of injuries that occurred. His vivid description of the injuries and care given illustrates the thoughts and skills of the author and the medical team. These patients were the same ages as many of our own brothers and sisters, and many of the nurses were just out of school. It was emotionally very difficult for many of the medical team to participate in the care of these young soldiers. Dr. Meffert's calming presence helped in difficult times.

"In addition, he made friends with the Vietnam doctors and was able to share his skills and knowledge with the physicians and staff at the provincial hospital. Even with minimal facilities, he performed sophisticated surgeries, including mitral valve heart surgeries, on carefully selected patients of the civilian population. These were performed at the evacuation hospital. His willingness to help the civilian population with the Vietnamese physicians reflects what medical care is all about. Many of these friendships continue today. It is physicians like Dr. William Meffert whose medical knowledge, skills, and caring qualities epitomize the very best in the medical profession.

"Thanks for the memories."

—Lenard L. Politte, MD, clinical professor of medicine, University of Missouri

"With cinematic sweep and focus, Dr. Meffert brings us to the precipice: we look hard and deep not only into mortal wounds but also into the war- and catastrophe-torn lives of those he cared for and worked with. With a surgeon's precision, drive, and economy, he masterfully explores connections, reveals the war's underbelly, and sews us whole."

—Audrey Shafer, professor emeritus, Department of Anesthesiology, Perioperative and Pain Medicine, Stanford University; and author of *The Mailbox*

THERE

WERE

NO

FLOWERS

THERE

A Surgeon's Story of War,

WERE

Family,

NO

and Love

FLOWERS

WILLIAM MEFFERT, MD

WGM Publishing House

Published by WGM Publishing House, Portola Valley, CA
www.williammeffertmd.com

Edited and designed by Girl Friday Productions
www.girlfridayproductions.com

Cover design: Megan Katsanevakis
Project management: Reshma Kooner
Editorial production: Abi Pollokoff
Image credits: cover © iStock/dikobraziy, iStock/Ales_Utovko

ISBN (paperback): 979-8-9859294-0-9
ISBN (e-book): 979-8-9859294-1-6

To Mimi, and our children: Stephen, Mollie, and Susan

It is quite true what philosophy says: That life must be understood backwards. But that makes one forget the other saying: That it must be lived—forwards. The more one ponders this, the more it comes to mean that life in the temporal existence never becomes quite intelligible, precisely because at no moment can I find complete quiet to take the backward-looking position.

—Søren Kierkegaard

CONTENTS

PROLOGUE

Clyde, the boy who would one day become my father, stands in front of his two taller brothers while scooping snow from the sidewalk in their small Iowa town. The steeply banked drift is higher than Clyde's head as he reaches up to throw a shovelful over the side, hands ungloved, a grim look on his face. Are his brothers teasing him for being so short? For being the youngest?

Their father, my grandfather, has just died from an ear infection; the family is destitute. Except for food from a vegetable garden and from the boys' hunting and fishing, they have nothing to eat. I thought about Dad growing up in the rural Iowa countryside, his life as a youngster and a young man, growing up dirt poor in an Iowa town with fewer than seven hundred people.

He and his brothers helped out by working at small jobs or by hunting and fishing. As a boy, Dad learned to scour the countryside on long walks, searching for pheasants, ducks, or even rabbits, and was an excellent shot with his rifle. On weekends, he worked as a clerk in a grocery store and after high school, spent several years as a salesman to earn money for college and medical school. He rarely travelled out of Iowa, and never saw an ocean before the war.

In 1920, when Clyde is almost twenty years old, he leaves home, flat broke, but works his way through college, medical school, and a surgical residency. For money, he walks the rural hills of Wisconsin in the summers, trying to get people interested in purchasing 3D viewers. Yellowed photographs show dust from gravel roads and the late-summer fields clinging to his perspiring face and clothing. His square-jawed good looks, prominent cheekbones, and hazel eyes shaded by a carefully creased fedora help him when he knocks on doors. He times the farm visits for early afternoon, when women might have a little spare time and men would be working in their fields. What farmer's wife would not be interested in buying? He has an honest face and a controlled neediness about him, but times are tough and money goes for seed, machinery, and livestock, not for looking at the Grand Canyon or Old Faithful in 3D. But Clyde persists.

"Everyone deserves the education from this viewer," he'd say, mopping the grime from his face. "It's almost like you are part of the photographs." After three years of selling and saving, he paid for college and medical school. He was tough.

It is no wonder that, years later, he was hard on me, his

only son, born when he was thirty-five years old. A photograph from 1942 shows Clyde in his army uniform, carrying a large duffel bag and boarding a train. He kneels to hug me, his nine-year-old-son, then shakes my hand before leaving for the war in Europe.

"Take care of the family, Bill."

It felt like being hit with a heavy club. I didn't know what he meant for me to do. I needed my dad. I hope he needed me too. Before he left for Europe, I went on surgical rounds with him on Sunday mornings. The emergency entrance we used at the city hospital was surrounded with bright lights and ambulances coming and going. We stepped aside while injured patients were rushed past us. Sometimes he took me to operating rooms at night to watch him perform emergency surgery.

"Just sit down on the floor if you feel faint."

When he said that, it seemed a challenge to me. Rather than sitting down, I looked away from the surgical site sometimes until my dizziness cleared. Often, Dad would have me enter a patient's room with him. I was usually shy and silent. But sometimes I would talk to a patient. I remember a bearded man, his face gouged from an accident, lying on his back in bed; there was a stale, sour smell, and the sheets were pulled up to his neck.

"Do you like motorcycles?" he asked me.

"Sure," I said, trying not to breathe too deeply.

Slowly he pushed the sheet aside, revealing a missing right leg and a large bloodstained bandage over what was just a stump. "Don't ever ride a motorcycle," he added.

When we would visit patients closer to my age, talking to them as they suffered from accidents or from recent surgery was especially difficult. But even at that age, I wanted to become a doctor. I never seriously thought about becoming anything else.

Years later, as a medical student, I recited the Hippocratic oath. Standing wide-eyed with a hundred other new doctors, innocent, even ignorant, I held my hand high. *First, do no harm.* The 1962 class of Yale medical school. It was simple. Problems were distant, faraway dreams. But six years later, I was a blood-and-sweat-soaked thoracic and vascular surgeon in a field hospital in Vietnam, waiting while orderlies scooped blood from the operating-room floor with snow shovels. What I saw changed the course of my life, and if I do my job right, this book will change yours too.

This is a story about what happens when you realize, as a surgeon, you are often responsible for people's lives and are forced to make decisions that will save or end their lives. It's about serious injuries and vascular closures demanding urgent, emergency surgery and deciding whether the unconscious patient would want to be saved only to be seriously debilitated or whether they would prefer not to live that life. What can we surgeons know about their thoughts, their family desires, and support? In war or civilian emergencies, we cannot speak with unconscious patients or to their relatives who are often thousands of miles away and still think their loved ones are healthy and safe from harm. These doctors must make life-and-death choices for patients and for families they have never met.

Surgeons, who must make these decisions, can never forget what happened. This explains why they, and many other veterans, do not talk about war or major trauma except to those who have experienced the uncontrolled hemorrhage of severe injuries, those who have been blinded by blood splashing on their faces or felt blood soaking scrub suits and spongy clots drying between their toes. No notes or diaries are necessary. Most of us can never forget what happened.

When I turned eighty-one, I realized that I needed to better understand Dad's life and my own. It might be my last chance to compare how we both, as surgeons, had survived the stress of our two wars, World War II and Vietnam. I wanted to get to know and understand him in a way I hadn't been able to when he was alive. How did those surgeons with Patton's army withstand the horrific scenes of so many dead and seriously wounded men from both sides? How did Dad manage mentally and physically? Did he, as I had, use endless surgery in the operating rooms to avoid contact with the screams and cries of arriving wounded soldiers?

Following his trail through Europe with Patton's army seemed like the best way to learn more about Dad as a surgeon and as a person. I wanted to learn more about the dangers he faced and how he reacted. Our son, Steve, a retinal surgeon with a calm disposition, came with me. He may have thought I needed the safety of his presence. (He was right!) It was wonderful to renew our closeness and to share the development of this book.

As a child, Steve had a different relationship than I did with Dad—a kind companion who, on walks through the countryside, taught him and our daughter Mollie about plants and animals while strolling nearby pastures. Steve and I collected stories about our tough and brave family, and stories of many courageous soldiers. We wanted to see the hospital tents, the surgical instruments, how wounds were managed, how soldiers arrived, and how they were discharged from harm's way. At my age, I thought it was our last chance for both of us to understand the determination of my father who, despite the obscene noises of armies fighting nearby and the shaking of flimsy medical tents from explosions, did his best to save lives of soldiers from both sides.

Then, two years later, we travelled together again to South Vietnam, collecting stories, comparing surgical treatments used in that war with those of World War II, and talking with people who had survived that war when I had been stationed in Da Nang fifty years ago.

This book shows rather than tells what happens. It is written by a surgeon who has been there, worked in many countries with trauma patients, and, despite many vivid memories about the effects of trauma on patients and families, remains optimistic about people and reverent about life.

THERE

WERE

NO

FLOWERS

FAMILY MOVES FROM IOWA
TO COLORADO (1941)

I was just a young kid when we moved from Iowa to a military base in Colorado for Dad's training. I had trouble learning to read in the new school and was confused and embarrassed. I had left all my Iowa friends. The old clapboard house we moved into was beside vegetable gardens cared for by German POWs. Every morning, these prisoners would arrive in large army trucks. I could hear them speaking German back and forth and listen to their soft laughing while I was still in bed. They wore white clothing with black stripes. Bending over with their knives, they harvested the vegetables, leaving them in piles that were later collected in carts. I had seen photographs of prisoners from other wars: the weakened bodies, the fear in their wrinkled, desperate faces. But these men talked freely back and forth, moved easily, and could have been working in their own gardens. They looked like us and not like the evil men I had seen in the movies.

Sometimes a few of my school friends and I would hold out sticks and pretend to shoot at them. The prisoners would laugh, point fingers, and pretend to shoot back. I liked them even though we were supposed to hate Nazis.

Everyone had jobs and little free time. Dad was gone for days as his hospital was put together. Mom worked part-time instructing high school students in physical education. People were going to factories and leaving for war. Tanks, jeeps, and huge guns crowded roads near our house; military aircraft landed and took off from a runway close to our school. We waved at them during recess. Some pilots waved back. Pikes Peak was dotted with black burn holes from plane crashes.

It felt like I had been planted in Colorado, another vegetable for the prisoners to care for. It felt like being naked. I had to start over. It was difficult to care for myself or anyone else because I didn't understand what I was being asked to do.

After a number of months, the hospital was fully operational and assigned to the Third Army in Europe.

Mom, my sister, and I stood with Dad in the dimly lit train depot the night he left for the war. Soldiers and their families crowded closely together. Outside, near the tracks, more khaki-dressed soldiers stood quietly in the cold. It was a foggy black night, just after midnight when we finally heard the rumbling of a train. After tears and kisses, Dad grasped my shoulder, and he and I left the depot together. Other soldiers, heads down and quiet, walked with us to the train, its dingy gray metal blending with the night. Dad looked down from the train steps:

"Take care of the family until I come home."

His voice was loud and clear. It felt like he had tossed me a heavy weight that took my breath away when I caught it. Then the train's whistle sounded twice and its wheels began to move.

I looked up to say, *Be careful!*, but he had stepped inside the train, already crowded with other soldiers. I looked into the windows but couldn't see him. I walked and then ran alongside, but the train gained speed and finally sank into the darkness.

I was too young to do what he wanted and too young to take his place. He probably wanted me to be older, to grow up faster. He was impatient. He tried to teach me to deal with problems as he had learned without a father.

As a young boy, I understood what he had told me to mean *If you don't succeed, you will be a failure and of little use to anyone.* But, as I write these memories down, I realize we were both facing unknowns. He was probably frightened to face the Nazis with their modern blitzkrieg army; I was scared that Dad might never return.

WORLD WAR II (1942–1945)

Dad's first letter to his family:

> Most of us have never been at sea before and
> many of us have never seen an ocean. Today is
> bright and clear, but looking in all directions,
> I see whitecaps, dark blue water, and no land,
> not even on the horizons.

Dad wrote this from the *Queen Mary* on the way to
England with his evacuation hospital in 1943. We worried
about German submarines, but the departure of military
ships was kept secret, and by the time his letter arrived,
he was in England. We had been told, or maybe I had seen
in a movie newsreel, that ships like the *Queen Mary* could
easily outrun any submarine. But even at age nine, I knew
that German submarines, the wolf packs, waited for ships
like my father's to come to them.

Later, on another ship, he wrote a letter describing
crossing the English Channel to Normandy:

> All the way across the English Channel it
> was choppy. Boats were pitching and yawing.
> Soldiers and hospital staff clung to the boat
> rails, vomiting. The sky was covered with air-
> craft, from one horizon to the other, each with
> stripes on the wings identifying them as ours.

Another letter from France:

> We haven't been anywhere I can write about.
> Now we have left Paris. Was able to walk up
> to the second platform of the Eiffel Tower. The
> elevator cables had been cut so Hitler couldn't
> ride to the top. Saw all of Paris from there. My
> gold major leaves have been changed to silver
> recently. Not much change, but now they call
> me "Colonel."

France; November 1944

> I think our mortality is the lowest of all the
> army hospitals, but we have been very lucky.
> Sometimes it is quite a struggle. We are begin-
> ning to receive more German wounded now.
> We like that because it means that our soldiers
> are moving forward. Received seven German
> soldiers with minor wounds yesterday who
> walked out of a nearby forest, waving a white
> flag.

Many of Dad's other letters were short like these. They
were read by censors and sometimes had black ink crossing out a few sentences.

After those months in Colorado, Mom, my sister, and
I had moved back to our home in Iowa to wait for Dad and
for whatever might happen.

After a few months of hard fighting, Patton's army entered Belgium. We knew that from news broadcasts. Mom was driving us to church on a Sunday, not far from our home. My sister sat in the front seat, reading Dad's latest letter. "It's from Bastogne!" she said. Then she looked at Mom and shouted, "Their hospital has been captured by the Germans!" My mother slammed on the brakes. "But not the patients, or the doctors and nurses," my sister continued, reading further. "They got away in time." Some of the letter had black censor marks over Dad's writing, so that was all we knew. We continued on to church.

The disruptions of Dad leaving for the war and the family's move to Colorado and then back to Iowa after he left for Europe interrupted my friendships and the happiness of earlier years in Iowa. It became difficult to concentrate in school. I was embarrassed to be put back one grade after we returned to Iowa because of difficulty learning to read. I remember the school principal, Miss Smithy, came during class to take me to the lower grade. While the other children watched, she helped pick up my papers, books, and pencils.

In the weeks before he left for Europe, Dad was especially hard on me and my sister. I don't entirely forgive him for prodding either of us with criticisms. I couldn't understand the urgency or the dangers approaching. What could he expect from a child? My parents taught me at an early age to concentrate on doing a good job with chores and to finish what I had started by putting things neatly away.

Perhaps they were premature in offering guidelines, but I can't blame them for wanting me to be more independent in those perilous, uncertain years. But that attitude made it more difficult for me in school.

Most of my friends were still in Iowa, but their fathers had also joined the army. We began spending time together. On Saturdays, we often took the bus downtown to the Paramount Theater to see double-feature movies. One Saturday morning, six of us were sitting close to the screen, eating popcorn and apples. The first movie was called *The Blonde from Singapore*. We liked the title, but it turned out disappointing because the actress played a missionary's daughter. Then there was a newsclip showing the herding of skeletal, cringing Jews and gypsies into cattle cars; photos of German soldiers forcing terrified children and adults into an airless mass before locking the railroad cars with wooden crossbars. Then, the evil, spastic face of Hitler, sweating, raising his arm to brush hair off his face, while shouting to thousands of cheering people who saluted when he told them to take over the world. We stood from our seats, booing and shouting at the movie screen until the lights came on and we had to leave.

My mother and her close friends sometimes whispered about the war and read censored mail after I went to bed. The silence and whispering downstairs below my bedroom made me think there was very bad news my sister, Molly, and I were not being told about—that the enemies were invading our country; maybe even they were at our city's edge. Sometimes I awoke in the dark, dreaming of German planes diving past our house, firing guns as they screamed past the windows.

Molly was a natural scholar in high school. She played the piano very well and didn't seem to worry. She kept on getting good grades and spent time with her friends; she consumed endless numbers of books but still had time for several boyfriends whom I water bombed from upstairs windows. She didn't often talk about Dad or when he might come home, except to Mom.

I mentioned that before Dad left for Europe, we had hunted together most weekends, searching for tracks along thick brush in the fall, looking for pheasants, and crunching through snow in the winter, even when it was below zero, looking for burrowed rabbits. Our feet and hands numb from the cold and Dad's eyebrows ice-covered from his frozen breath, we would talk and smile as wind-driven snow caked both of us. Neither of us would admit the painful cold or talk about heading back to the truck. I really missed him. I suppose it's partially excusable that I was strict with our children after growing up with my father. Perhaps I was subconsciously imitating him.

Maybe war experiences also caused unnecessary strictness in my family. Thankfully, my wife, Mimi, while supporting most household rules, showed more common sense.

"Call us if for some reason you can't be home on time. I don't want you speeding to avoid being home late and perhaps being in a car accident."

However, she could even be more inventive with our children than I ever was. She told Steve he had to get a job if he was staying home during the summer after his first year in college. When he didn't, she got him a job digging irrigation ditches on a Montana ranch and presented him with bus tickets.

***

Stephen became an excellent retinal surgeon. Now fifty-five years old, he had urged me five years ago to take him back to where I had served as an army surgeon in Vietnam. But bloody memories were still too distinct for me to go on that trip. I suggested instead we retrace my father's surgical experiences in World War II as the chief surgeon in the 109th Evacuation Hospital in General Patton's Third Army. We would see if that stirred up too many nightmares. After careful reading about that war and detailed planning to visit battle sites, museums, and cemeteries in Europe, we set out. After years of busy schedules, but now travelling together along my father's course in his war, Steve and I also shared memories of living in Iowa.

It was a beautiful October day in 2018 when Steve and I arrived in Normandy and stood on Omaha Beach where my father's hospital had come ashore seventy-five years earlier. The gently curved sandy beach extended for ten miles with only a few remnants of the crossed iron barriers, once armed with deadly explosives that blocked American tanks and landing craft. To us, it looked like a pleasant tourist destination with a few small cafés, hard-surfaced roads, and walking pathways close to the ocean's edge. A breeze, too gentle to stir the sand, slowly moved flags marking landing sites and pathways to the flat bluffs farther inland. Small yellow butterflies fluttered silently around clustered wildflowers. It was very quiet. The dead and dying had been scattered where we now stood at the edge of a Normandy farm less than a mile from the ocean. The land, gently rolling, resembled the fertile hills of Iowa. Looking at the destruction near his hospital above Omaha Beach, I think he must have thought he would not return home and had to be frightened. Perhaps that's why he spoke those words to me the night he headed for war.

Memories of my parents had slowly receded in my mind. Steve's memories of his grandparents were sharper and different from mine. My wife, with our two children, returned to Iowa and lived with both sets of our parents while I was in Vietnam. They saw my parents almost every day. My mother read to Stephen often and rubbed lotion on his hands during the coldest times that winter. Dad often walked with our children through the countryside. He showed Steve and Mollie how snapping turtles survived under iced rivers, how pheasants and rabbits stayed warm in the winter, and how many animals changed colors for breeding and safety. When I was in Vietnam, Dad became like a kind father to our children. They seldom argued. It was the relationship I had wanted with my dad instead of always the challenges and the setting of goals. It would have been wonderful to have had a kinder, gentler relationship with him. He may have felt that way, too, but that came later for both of us.

During this trip to examine Dad's war experiences, as Steve and I stood together about a mile from Normandy Beach, I asked him, "You two got along just fine, didn't you?"

He turned from looking at the dark arc of ocean a mile away.

"Grandpa seemed most comfortable outdoors. We would start walking slowly, not knowing what would happen or what we might find; capturing a snapping turtle or even burning a dead cow. He could point to four-leaf clovers as we walked through the fields."

Then he looked again at the faded photograph of Dad's hospital showing the khaki-colored tents and soldiers in dark uniforms.

"I didn't know him when he was a surgeon. But I remember his deerskin work gloves with drawstrings at the wrist, so worn that they would stand on their own like half-closed fists. His scuffed brown work boots stood by the door. His mustard-colored pickup truck filled with old tools and walking sticks, always one cut the right length for friends and family."

Then Steve turned to me. "I remember you were tough on us when you had a busy surgical schedule. No phone calls after eight in the evening. Curfews on the weekends and of course no alcohol or smoking. Remember the time you pulled me out of that house party about midnight? The physical fight we had?"

"There weren't any lights on, and the place smelled like a brewery. I thought of it more like a rescue," I answered.

"Well, you have changed since you retired. You have mellowed. Grandpa must have also."

I laughed softly. "Must be in the genes."

I had missed much of the nurturing from my father that our children had received. My dad and I were competitors and companions from my childhood until his death at age ninety-two. Our times together were often intense even before he left for Europe.

"Don't tie a knot like that," he'd say, watching his kid tie a hook to a fishing line. He pulled the knot open easily. "It's a granny," he said. "Tie a square knot, like this." His hands moved too rapidly for me. "Now tie a square knot." But I couldn't without further help. "Well, I showed you. You sit there until you get it," he said, and continued walking along Buffalo Creek.

In a few years, it was who was a better shot, who could walk the farthest in a freezing blizzard, or who had been the better wrestler, and finally, who was the better surgeon. We seldom talked except when I went to hospitals with him or when he looked at my report card.

There was no doubt that he was gifted, energetic, stubborn, and tough. I saw him express tenderness and compassion with his patients, but I thought he had a hard time expressing love and sometimes seemed to lack appreciation for his family.

For me, it was a tough love, and our long, unrelenting competition gave me a determination, not unlike his own, to make the best efforts to do things well.

But maybe it wasn't too late to learn about the other side of my father from Steve. I suppose Steve and Mollie felt the same about me as I thought about Dad. I was gone to war, gone to a hospital, gone to meetings and conferences, just gone. Perhaps I had been too strict with them as well as too distant. Now I wanted to know both Dad and my children better. I hoped Steve had similar feelings. Searching the pathway of Patton's army, it seemed that Dad, Steve, and I were together trying to better understand each other.

I hoped I had shared love with my children in more obvious ways than my father was able to share with me. And perhaps this was my last chance to share yet untold memories of my dad and mom with the younger generation.

I thought our children should know how hard our parents had worked and how much they had sacrificed to help others and to encourage our successful education. How many people, like my mother, would have left their home on an Iowa farm, gone to college, and earned a master's degree from Columbia University in New York? Not many would have spent two years as a travelling salesman like my father had, often parking his car to save money and walking the dusty farm roads, pitching 3D viewers to earn his way through college and medical school. Our children should know about the determination of their grandparents, the strong, courageous lives they lived, and what previous generations had done for them.

***

The next day in Normandy, Steve and I rode in a lumbering black van along a graveled pathway leading from the beach past wrecked tanks, blown-out machine-gun posts, caved trenches, and destroyed German heavy guns. Stopping the van, Gwenael, our guide, pointed to a flat field above the beach.

"The hospital was right there," he said. He and Steve, walking to the American hospital site, easily jumped across an old German trench. I jumped after them but couldn't make the other side. I started falling. Suddenly a hand, Steve's, reached out and pulled me over the trench. He was looking out for me. When did he start that? Grateful, I hadn't noticed the transition from years of me looking after him.

I looked at the farm field planted with closely spaced green corn and long, narrow fields of recently cut hay. A faded American flag waved above us. Milking cows grazed peacefully, quiet except for their brawling in nearby pastures. In 1944, their battle-slaughtered ancestors had shared the littered landscape with dead soldiers, destroyed German machinery, and gun emplacements. Dad's hospital was first placed on this bluff above the beach less than a mile from the ocean. There was a small photograph encased in plastic and fastened to a faded wooden marker at the edge of a cornfield. The aerial photograph showed rows of tents and a nearby dirt landing field that had been used by aircraft to evacuate patients to England and by American P-38 fighters needing emergency landings. The hospital's tents had opened to that airfield.

We may have stood exactly where Dad stood in 1944, chief of surgery in the American hospital with the lowest mortality in World War II. I felt weak, hardly able to move and unable to hold back tears. It seemed to me that my father was standing there with us. Looking at the scarred remnants of the army hospital, I could see Dad working on a wounded soldier. He stood at an unstable operating room table that rocked back and forth. The savage artillery explosions, the roaring of strafing aircraft, the shouting and screaming medics and wounded soldiers. How could precise surgery have taken place? Small surgical lights, mounted high above the operating tables, provided only a dim view of wounds. All hospital equipment was folded up and put on trucks every few weeks to stay with Patton's army. Winds and storms blew easily through the surgical tents. There were no antibiotics and only blood for transfusions.

The Normandy field Steve and I stood on was just above Omaha Beach. The wrecked gun emplacements with collapsed layers of concrete and rusted, twisted guns still looked lethal and dangerous even seventy-five years after those guns had killed thousands of allied soldiers. The machine-gun bunkers, the tunnels, and trenches would have hidden the enemy. Dad had to be physically and mentally tough to survive this. Paying for his own education took several years and explained why he was in his forties when he volunteered to enter the army.

Twenty-five years after my dad was in Normandy, I became a combat surgeon in Vietnam. I was twenty-nine years old after completing medical school and six years of surgical training. Well trained but very inexperienced in trauma surgery.

Instead of tents, our hospital was constructed of Quonset buildings; the operating tables were fixed in concrete. There was excellent surgical lighting; antibiotics were plentiful; and we seldom ran out of blood for transfusions. Helicopter evacuation of wounded soldiers within thirty minutes of their injury was not unusual. In previous wars, many soldiers bled to death before reaching hospitals. Vascular repair, rare in my father's time, was common in Vietnam. But we didn't move with an army, and no battle lines between armies existed. The enemy was often right beside us, making travel to Vietnamese hospitals through Da Nang risky.

***

Steve and I continued to follow Patton's army's progress through the countryside of Belgium to the city of Bastogne. I never found out exactly where Dad's hospital was located there. Whether it had been in or just near the town, we didn't know. They were constantly on the move and perhaps if outside Bastogne, didn't know where they were themselves. I never knew before why the Germans didn't just bypass Bastogne on their way to Antwerp during their offensive. Now I understood. The town is in the Ardennes Forest. During the war, only narrow roads wound through closely spaced trees and underbrush, finally converging at Bastogne. The weather that winter was terrible with record-low temperatures, heavy snow, and ice storms. Travelling off-road through the few fields cleared of trees was impossible with mud, icing, and deep snow waiting to disable the large German tanks and artillery. The Germans had to use the roads near Bastogne in order to continue their blitzkrieg. But they were stopped a few miles west of Bastogne after failing to capture the city and failing to capture fuel for their tanks and heavy mobile guns.

The fighting was desperate, the outcome uncertain. Patton's army fought its way into the city. American tanks burst through the German lines with all guns firing and entered Bastogne before the enemy had time to react.

"I believe it is appointed to each man to have a few minutes of glory in his life," the tank commander said after the war. "Mine lasted four miles and twenty-five minutes."

But heavy fighting continued in surrounding villages, and even the fringes of Bastogne were not yet secured. The fighting lasted five tense weeks. We listened to news broadcasts compulsively and learned of shocking numbers of casualties. Finally, the Germans abandoned almost all of their irreplaceable armor and artillery pieces after exhausting their gasoline. Many retreated by walking back to Germany.

Army hospitals must have been overwhelmed. Many injured were unable to get even first aid because of the intense fighting. They just froze to death in place. If the wounded arrived at army hospitals, they were triaged. Some with multiple severe injuries were not taken to surgery but were given narcotics for comfort.

I thought about my dad. It must have been very depressing for him to see so many dead soldiers beyond help, lying frozen in the snow, and having to triage those badly injured but still alive with the comfort of morphine instead of surgery. It was against his training, against the physician's oath to preserve and to offer comfort to those in need.

GERMANY AND IOWA (1945)

Dad's letters from Germany:

> We never have much contact with the German civilians. We have wrecked their towns in fighting their army, and that's ok with me. By their looks, we know they don't like us very much. But the people the Germans have enslaved and who are now free are really happy.
>
> Love, Dad

Germany; April 10, 1945

Not as many wounded now that the Germans are definitely licked. They try to hold out in places but really get pounded whenever they stop. Saw one of their large towns yesterday. Unbelievable. No buildings were left standing.

Met up with the Russians last week. There were toasts to the Russian Motherland, toasts to Patton's army, toasts to being alive, toasts to little children, and finally, maybe, toasts to toasts, I don't remember. Several of us drank olive oil to coat our stomachs before we reached their lines to slow the absorption of their vodka. Finally, the Russians just sat in their chairs watching us drive away in our jeeps, still feeling ok because of the oil protecting our stomachs. Slept quite well that night.

Can't find anything to send to Bill for his birthday, but many German tanks and other weapons are just abandoned or lying discarded on the ground. I found a German Mauser rifle in good condition and I'm sending it for Bill. I know he's not old enough yet, but someday maybe we can go hunting with it and shoot a deer.

Those splashes on the letter are drops

of rain coming through the top of the tent
around the stovepipe.

Love, Dad

***

There was a map of Europe on a wall of our Iowa kitchen
and a small portable radio on a counter near the stove.
While Dad was gone, we ate meals at a small folding table
nearby and listened to the nightly news about the war.
Redheaded pins pressed into the map followed Patton's
army. We talked about Dad's latest letters, and Mom would
ask us to write him at least once a week, often suggesting
things we might include.

Mom usually knew what we were doing, where we were,
and assigned me certain jobs like mowing and trimming
the yard in the summers, and shoveling winter snow from
the driveway. She was red haired and energetic with a great
sense of humor. She was always optimistic, but not satisfied without maximum efforts when it came to important
objectives. We enjoyed exploring hardware stores together,
and I helped her fix leaky faucets. She must have thought I
needed another talent other than doing chores. I remember
her asking me if I would like to play a musical instrument.
I must have been equivocal in my answer. Actually, I was
attracted to the trumpet. But she borrowed a clarinet from
one of her relatives and signed me up for classical music
lessons. When playing musical instruments, it helps to like
doing it and to enjoy the music you are practicing. I liked

pop music. After a year or so, the music teacher told me I was wasting my parents' money and my time. Oh, what a happy day that was. I also disliked the marching band, especially during the halftimes of frigid football games, when my clarinet reed froze to the mouthpiece no matter how hard I blew into the thing. People at the games held their fingers to their ears to avoid the insane squeaking as the wind-instrument section marched past them. I told Mom they were giving us the finger. Mom took the clarinet to the attic, and I went out for wrestling. But forcing the clarinet on me was about her only failure.

She provided a solid foundation for both my sister and me during those years of uncertainty. She took us to church regularly; we said prayers for our soldiers' safety, prayers that the war would end soon, and prayers that Dad would soon return. Relatives and neighbors visited us frequently, I suppose just to check on us and perhaps learn more about the latest war news from Dad's letters.

The gift from Dad for my birthday, the Mauser rifle, arrived at our home when Mom was running errands, perhaps buying rationed groceries with her coupons. The heavy metal box had been cut open by censors and closed with shipping tape. I eagerly ripped open the box, receiving numerous cuts on my right hand from the jagged metal edges. I got a few towels from a nearby bathroom to keep blood off the carpet. The gun parts were wrapped in a bloodstained Nazi flag. I laid the oily gun parts on our living-room floor with no idea how they might fit together. Mom came home about then and looked at my hand. I remember how well she managed unexpected things like those cuts. I look at those scars seventy years later. The cuts must have been deep to heal with such prominent scarring. I remember the sting as the metal sliced my hand, but Mom just covered the cuts with bandages and, except for changing them a few times, let nature do the healing.

Neither one of us had any idea how to put the gun together. Just as confused with all the gun parts as I was, she called Dr. Jankowski, a Polish doctor who had recently begun practicing in town after escaping from a German prison camp, to ask for help putting the Mauser together. It was an early-winter evening when he arrived. Tall and serious, with lots of swept-back dark hair, he had very prominent white teeth. "I am Dr. Jan-cow-skiiii," he said with a slight whistle. Mom later said the teeth were replacements put in by a dentist she had recommended. His teeth had been knocked out by German soldiers. He escaped from Poland by walking to Italy. The doctor assembled the gun quickly and held it to his shoulder several times while talking with my mother in our kitchen, which was only a few feet away from the Wilsons' house next door. I could see them staring at us through their windows. Their lights were still on after Dr. Jankowski left our house amid handshakes and a few kisses. I had never been kissed by a man before. Mrs. Wilson called Mom early the next morning to tell her that they saw this large man pointing a gun around our house and thought they should call the police.

"But we watched for a while and both you and the gunman were smiling. Neither one of us had ever seen a *holdup* with so much talking and smiling, don't you know, so we didn't call for help. I never slept all night, wondering if we should have, though."

Mom thanked her, wrapped the gun in a cotton blanket, and stood it upright beside the dresser in her bedroom. I never saw the Nazi flag again.

She enrolled my sister Molly and me in more difficult courses in our school and never missed parent-teacher meetings about our progress. She threw away newspapers containing bad war news. And years later, when the time came, she insisted that we apply to the best colleges and universities.

Germany; April 21, 1945

> Dear family,
>   Don't know yet whether we will get to come home after this is finished or go over and help in the Pacific, but anyway one of these days it will be finished altogether. I have a German shepherd now. He's a lot of company, but almost as stubborn as Bill— or as I am. Anyway, we get along ok.

Pilsen, Czechoslovakia; June 27, 1945

> Dear family,
>   Not much to write about. I haven't had any mail for a long time. Very little work.

No more fighting, but we stay prepared and ready for whatever. All of us, of course, wonder what will happen now. Looks as if we may be here for several months. Will probably miss Mom's birthday next October. May be transferred to the Pacific to help over there. Whatever it takes, one day it will all be over and we will come back home.

Bill, I have been getting some good reports about you. Your schoolwork is very good. I hope you also are not too difficult for Mom to handle.

Several months before Dad's letter, my mathematics teacher, Miss Cory, had me sit down to go over a few algebra papers of mine. Looking up from the math, she smiled and said, "This is really good work."

I looked at her. Her eyes were focused on me. She was serious. She meant what she said.

"You can be an excellent student too."

That afternoon, something changed inside me. Maybe I was just ready; maybe a psychiatrist would have a better answer or a theory. It was just that comment she made. I thought it was a sincere compliment. Before then, comments from teachers about my academic performance were rare. I eventually became a serious student and developed a new measure of self-confidence because of the time she had taken with me. As the years passed, I often thought about what she had said. I began to work hard in school, getting As in courses except for a C– in penmanship. My sister, a beautiful writer as well as an excellent student, was shocked at my C–.

"How could you get a grade like that?" she asked.

Miss Dimsdale was my relentless, dour handwriting teacher. Even now, I can hear her heavy leather footsteps coming up behind me to check if I had made any progress. I never told my parents or my sister about getting on my bike one day in the school parking lot. Moving the handlebars, I realized how strong the sun's reflection from my bike's large mirror was when it accidentally flashed across a nearby school wall. I parked my bike and turned the mirror so its reflection blasted into Miss Dimsdale's classroom. One of my friends, shielding his eyes with his hand, shouted from the classroom window that she wanted to see me in her room after school. That time, I had to write *Kansas produces wheat* one hundred times on the blackboard. There were a few other disagreements with her during that semester. Some of us developed realistic farts by trapping air under our arms before suddenly releasing it. Another of my friends, with especially bad penmanship, developed a deep, wet nauseating belch after considerable practice during recess, sometimes provoking a stampede of students out of the room. In the process, my friends and I learned more about Kansas.

Somehow my mother eventually found out about all this. Some things I just tried to suppress, but she knew about it and talked to me one day when we were working outdoors together.

"You need to settle down in your penmanship class. There are just a few weeks left before this semester ends."

It was an almost humorous warning. I remember her slight smile. "Try not to make any more trouble," she said, then continued. "Anyway, what you write is much more important than how you write it."

I had wanted a dog for a long time—any dog. When I saw the German shepherd standing beside my dad in a photograph he sent us, I wrote him a letter asking if I could have a dog for my next birthday. A dog would be a great companion. I could teach him lots of tricks. When Dad returned, we could take the dog hunting with us. I was almost certain he would agree—especially with the hunting idea.

Several weeks later, another letter arrived from Germany:

> Bill,
>
> Thanks for the letter. The shepherd dog just showed up at our hospital several months ago. I have no idea where he came from. He was wild-eyed then, his ribs were showing, and he was easily frightened by loud gunfire. I fed him, not too much at first, but then more later. He became my guard dog who would go on walks and move between me and any strangers we happened to meet.
>
> I think you are old enough for a dog. If

you choose a small one, it can be just yours.
If you choose a larger dog, it should belong
to the family.
    Dad

I didn't understand that last sentence. What difference did size make about having a dog for my own? Was it a test to see if I was selfish? Even now, I'm not certain why he said that, but he knew I loved large dogs and, I guess, wanted to see if I would choose a small one just for me, or share a larger dog that the entire family could enjoy and care for. Several of my cousins lived on nearby farms and owned large dogs. They were pets, but also guard dogs who kept predators like foxes and coyotes away from the chickens and other small animals. Those dogs were companions, but they were also useful. That's what I wanted. A large, useful dog like Lassie in the movies. I hadn't thought about myself owning a dog; I was planning to have any size dog be part of our family.

Laddie was a puppy who quickly became a full-sized collie and looked like Lassie in the movies. We all loved him and taught him commands and tricks. Even running hundreds of yards away and hearing "Stop," he would immediately sit down. "Roll over," and he would immediately roll over. I thought he loved Mom, Molly, and me the same, but then Dad came home. In the evenings, when Mom let Laddie into our house, he would run, tail wagging like an airplane propeller, into the living room where Dad sat in his chair with an open newspaper. Even if Dad was asleep,

Laddie would wag his tail before lying quietly on the floor beside him. Molly, Mom, and I took care of Laddie for months before Dad returned from Europe. I never understood how Laddie sensed that Dad was the family leader.

BACK FROM EUROPE

When Dad returned from the war, he was quiet, seemed older, and quickly became busy taking care of patients and doing surgery. We didn't talk as much or go hunting as often as before the war. It was as if we were all stunned after surviving a raging flood and somehow our family had managed now to be in calm water, a back pool for the moment, trying to protect each other from the violent river still nearby. He usually slept in his chair before and after dinner between phone calls. He left home early in the mornings and returned after dark. Thinking about it after my Vietnam experience, I believe he was using his busy practice, his long hours in operating rooms and in his office, to crowd out war memories. One day, I'd do the same after Vietnam.

***

Dad rarely talked about his experiences as a combat surgeon. I remember asking him about Colonel Prazak, who was the chief of Dad's hospital and a close friend of our family when we lived in Colorado. I tried to get talk about surgery started.

"How's Dr. Prazak?"

"Why are you asking me? It all happened long ago. George died last year."

Then I remembered several months ago Dad talked about George being sick. Dad went to see him but didn't talk about the visit either. He told me a few short war stories that he and George might have shared or that might have been fixed permanently in his memory.

"We only did what we had to do. You should have seen the beat-up German wounded: shoes missing, uniforms ripped, wounds filled with dirt and badly infected. We had to watch our Polish and Czechoslovakian hospital workers—the ones that had been German slaves who had somehow escaped. After being tortured and starved, they wanted to kill the German patients, especially the Nazi SS troops. Why are you asking me this now?"

He left the room rather than talk more about his war experiences, and I never understood why until I returned home after serving as a combat surgeon in Vietnam. How can you talk about the dead, the torn bodies, and the desperate surgery without pulling unwanted memories out of your mind and reopening pathways to the horror that had slowly faded through the years?

I easily recall helicopters crowding together on the helipad—each one unloading three or four wounded and dead GIs. Larger double-rotor Chinook helicopters could each unload twenty wounded soldiers. The admissions ward sometimes held fifty wounded who were rapidly triaged; the most seriously wounded and unstable were rushed to surgery. There might be a GI in shock with intestines hanging from the abdomen and mutilating injuries to both legs from a mine blast; another soldier might be unconscious with part of his chest wall missing; another might have an arm attached only with tissue shreds and bleeding from large shoulder blood vessels. We had one chance to help and had to think rapidly. Which injury threatened most? Which one should be treated first? Stop the bleeding wherever it might be coming from. Stop it or lose the soldier.

It's impossible to forget these patients. In my mind, they are covered only by a thin veneer of time. Words of explanation to innocent questions make nightmares start once again. Talk of the "heroes" who fled to Canada rather than serve in Vietnam brings sharp visions of wounded and dead GIs who fought in their place.

My father must have had very similar memories. He never talked much about the war, and after retirement, liked the solitude of long walks in the Iowa countryside and a stiff drink of Scotch in the evenings.

***

Despite Dad's letters during the war, I had little idea what he actually did in the operating rooms as a surgeon, so I asked him to take me with him on emergencies after he returned home and resumed his surgical practice. The first time, Dad took me with him to see a boy my age in a small country hospital. A family doctor had called in the middle of the night.

I remember seeing this boy in severe pain because something was wrong inside his abdomen. It was three or four in the morning when surgery began. Like a small ghost, wrapped in white scrubs, I sat on a seat at the head of the operating-room table with the anesthetist and helped pour ether. There was a view inside the opened abdomen: the intestines and the infected appendix that my father showed the gowned father standing behind him.

Dad, I suppose, thought a family member would be interested in seeing why their child was ill. But I started sweating and several times had to stare at the floor to avoid fainting, but each time I got up and returned to the shiny metal seat beside the anesthetist.

"Why show them?" I asked afterward.

"It helps them understand," Dad said. "Anyway, they're used to seeing animals' insides. They live on farms."

After the operation, he talked to the mother and father, who couldn't pay for surgery. My father held their hands and told them not to worry about the bill because he was not going to send one. Driving back home before sunrise, we talked about why he became a surgeon.

"Taking care of people always comes first—even before church, holidays, or parties. I think it's handy sometimes, especially if you're lacking sleep from night emergencies. You take a short nap and then show up at parties or holiday get-togethers when you can or when you want to and don't have to worry about being late."

I remember many times, he never showed up at all.

When I was a young boy, at parties, or after church, Dad was often still at the hospital.

Mornings he left for work before I was awake, and evenings he usually slept on the couch before and after dinner.

Until he started taking me to hospitals, I didn't really know much about him. Night emergencies, when most people were sleeping and voices had an urgent sharpness, were the most exciting. Being a doctor and driving a fast car seemed unreal to me then. How could you start as just a kid and one day become someone who could save lives and drive as fast as you wanted?

"Well, you'll see, honey," my mom said when we talked about it. "Not much in life happens suddenly. You'll just figure out what you want to do and then work on it each day. You can do anything you want if you work hard." My lips moved with hers. I had that last sentence memorized. She always offered me her warm support and encouragement.

I asked Mom how I could spend more time with Dad. She must have talked with him, because a few nights later he stood beside my bed at one o'clock in the morning.

"Bill, I've got to go see a patient in Monticello. She's having a lot of pain in her stomach; may have to operate on her. Want to come along?"

Our old brick house faded away in the headlights as we backed down the driveway. We were soon racing along in my dad's big white Cadillac, way over the limit. Then he really opened it up on the narrow highway leading to Monticello, the centerline stripes rushing by in a blur. This car was new, with wide leather seats and electric windows instead of cranks. The bumper guards looked like large bullets, and chrome stripes ran along the doors and fenders to the tail fins. A large chrome V was on the front and rear. It went like hell.

Dad floored it, and soon the wind was screaming even louder than the engine. I watched the white speedometer needle move rapidly to the right—60, 70, 80, 90, 100. "There's a three-mile straight stretch after this next curve," he said, red-tipped cigarette moving up and down as he talked. "Don't be surprised at the bouncing when we go over a little bridge a mile ahead." Foot to the floor, leaning forward, both hands gripping the wheel—90, 100, 110, we flew across the narrow wooden bridge and through the black night surrounded by warm odors of farm animals and the sweet smell of freshly cut hay.

We slowed for the last curve before Monticello and passed by blinking red neon, "Eat Gas 24 Hours," then coasted through deserted streets to a tall white building on a hill, Henderson Hospital. The Henderson family had given their home to the town for a hospital after the kids moved away. As we drove up the curving driveway, the headlights dimly showed a towering mansion with windowed turrets and dark balconies. It looked haunted.

Dr. Meyers was standing under the light near the front stairs. He was sort of stooped over with small round glasses. He smiled.

"My God, that didn't take long, Clyde," he said, shaking hands. "Didn't I just talk to you about half an hour ago?"

"No other cars," my dad said as we walked up the steep

stairs and through the large double entrance doors. "I brought my son, Bill, with me."

"Glad you did," Dr. Meyers said, holding the handrail, carefully taking one step at a time. "Can't start them too early. You'll have an interesting time tonight, son."

"Yes, sir," I said, still listening to the crinkling, cracking sounds of the hot Cadillac. Maybe I could just sleep in the car while they took care of the problem. But Dr. Meyers had his hand on my shoulder and the car was behind us. There were very few lights as we walked up a winding staircase to the second floor and past a life-sized statue of Jesus with his arms reaching out, eyes staring up at heaven, folds of blue and yellow robes lit by several candles at his feet. Dr. Meyers carried a flashlight as we walked along the dark hallway to the patient's room. I followed along behind like a useless wooden toy being towed by a string.

I stopped at the doorway but watched closely as the two doctors entered. Looking over the tops of his glasses, Dr. Meyers introduced my dad.

"Here is Dr. Meffert. I called him to come up and take a look. Clyde, this is Marian Clark in bed and Jake Clark beside her."

I could see Mrs. Clark, white as a wax candle, holding her belly, and Jake standing there looking scared as hell, his white wrinkled forehead contrasting with a deeply tanned face, his sun-darkened hands clasped together.

"Tell us what happened," Dr. Meyers said.

"Well, I was just usual until yesterday. Then I had a little pain right here." Mrs. Clark pointed low on her stomach.

"It got a lot worse this evening, and when I got up from the chair after dinner, I fainted; didn't I, Jake?"

"You sure did. Scared the hell out of me, honey."

"Any nausea or vomiting or diarrhea?"

"Just a little nausea."

"Any fever?"

"No."

"Have you ever had these problems before?"

"No."

"Are your periods normal?" Dad asked.

"No. I've missed the last two."

Dad touched her belly. She grabbed his hands and shouted, "Oh, Doc, that hurts like hell. Don't press on it!" She turned on her side and brought up her knees.

I bit my lip and looked at the floor; never saw anyone in that much pain before.

Dad turned to Dr. Meyers.

"Well, Alex, looks like she's got bleeding in her abdomen, don't you think? Her missed periods make me concerned about a tubal or abdominal pregnancy."

"The laboratory studies show severe anemia. I sent for some blood in case she needs a transfusion."

"We need to look in there," Dad said. "Shouldn't wait for morning, and we should do it here rather than wait for an ambulance. How about anesthesia and a scrub nurse?"

"We have two nurses on call and sterile instruments upstairs. I can give an ether anesthetic."

The operating room was on the fourth floor. Mrs. Clark was carried on a stretcher up the two flights of stairs and down another dim hallway, Dr. Meyers holding the front handles, my dad at the rear. I walked behind again. Everything smelled like bleach. The floor squeaked.

We came to a small white room with a bright overhead light where two nurses were laying out instruments and opening packages of gauze sponges. Mrs. Clark was moved carefully from the stretcher onto a metal table in the operating room. Then the two doctors and I walked to the nearby dressing room.

"Alex, is it ok with you if Bill watches?"

"Hell yes," he answered, pulling on his white scrub suit. I looked through the tall stack of uniforms for the smallest size.

"Oh, don't worry about size," my dad said. "We'll just roll up the sleeves and pant cuffs and pin the waist so they don't fall off. Here, put on this cap. I'll tie this mask around your neck." I stood there trying to get enough air through the heavy mask while the two of them began scrubbing their hands. They looked comfortable in their white clothes and masks. I could see through the window into the operating room as Mrs. Clark's gown was removed and she was painted with iodine. She was the first naked woman I had ever seen before except my mother once by accident. So pale and so quickly painted orange, her body didn't seem real. White sheets were put over her, covering everything except the stomach. Dr. Meyers started the anesthetic. He motioned to me to come into the operating room. I loosened my mask a little and entered the room but stayed against the wall. One of the nurses turned to me, eyes narrowed above her mask. "Don't touch any-thing!" she said. I put my hands behind me and stood there in the bright white room, fingers locked and sweaty, not sure of what to do. Another nurse and my dad stepped up to the patient's side.

"She's ready, Clyde," Dr. Meyers said.

"Scalpel!" A nurse handed my dad this little shiny knife that he pressed against the patient's skin. Blood flowed from the cut. "Hemostat, silk, sponge, hold the retractor like this," Dad said, pulling on the handle and looking up at the nurse. Sometimes he talked to me like that, espe-cially when I was trying to tie a knot or fix something that was broken. "That's the wrong way," he would say, and then leave the room. Later my mom and I would figure out how to do it.

I looked away, thinking how great the trip home in the Cadillac would be.

"Bill, come over here," Dr. Meyers said, again looking over his glasses. He was sitting on a shiny metal stool near the patient's head. "See how I pour this ether?" He was holding a metal can about the size of a Campbell's Soup can my mother used in our kitchen. He had cut off the small top and put in a cork with a small *V* cut in it. Ether dripped from a short piece of pipe cleaner stuck through the notch onto a soft mask held over Mrs. Clark's face.

His wrinkled, hairy hand held the mask firmly.

"She breathes it, and it keeps her asleep. You just have to be careful not to drip too much or too little. You have to listen to how she breathes. Sit here beside me on my chair," he said, moving to the edge of the round seat. "I'll hold your wrist. You hold the can. There you go. Just go round and round the mask. Listen to her breathe." He had a calm voice and explained things much better than my dad.

Mrs. Clark sounded like she had just been frightened by Frankenstein. You know how girls do watching movies, only she did it over and over. Her forehead started to frown.

"That's not enough. See; she's waking up." I poured more out of the can, and her breathing deepened but then became softer.

"See; that's too much!"

I tipped the can back but dripped some on my pants. It was cold and smelled like mothballs. I liked it. Dr. Meyers took over.

About then my dad asked for the suction. I stood up and saw all the blood rushing through the plastic tubing into a large bottle on the floor. Sponges were soaked with blood. "Alex, you better start a unit of blood," my dad said, looking through the cut into Mrs. Clark's abdomen.

I didn't know we had that much blood in us. The glass bottle on the floor was half-full of Mrs. Clark's blood! Jesus! In the movies, people get hurt, bleed just a little, and fall over. But no one seemed too worried except me.

"I've got it," Dad said. He had one of his gloved hands around something deep inside her. "Have Jake come in so I can show him what the problem is." I had no idea people were hollow inside—that you could reach inside them to fix things.

In a few minutes, Mr. Clark came wide-eyed into the

operating room through a glass side door, his overalls and boots partly covered by a small white gown a nurse was trying to tie around his chest.

"Jake, step up on the stool behind me," my dad said. Silently, his eyes staring above his mask, Jake stepped up and put a hand against my dad's back to steady himself.

"She bled quite a lot. See this red thing here?" Mr. Clark leaned forward; he was sweating. Dad turned his head to look at him.

"Easy, Jake; don't push any harder. Don't want you to fall into us. Is he ok, Nurse?"

"Hell, I'm ok, Doc. Just something you don't see every damn day."

"It's about the size of a walnut. It's a pregnancy that never made it down Marian's right tube to her uterus. It got stuck in the tube and started to grow, got larger, and finally broke open and bled into her abdomen."

Dr. Meyers was dripping the ether now; I was standing beside him so I could see what Mr. Clark was looking at. Dad had a red thing between his fingers of his left hand; small spurts of blood shot out with each heartbeat. He put two clamps just under his fingers, and the bleeding stopped. He cut between the clamps and lifted the red thing out of Mrs. Clark.

"Here it is," he said, holding the thing carefully before handing it to the nurse beside him. "I forgot to ask how many kids you have, Jake."

"Two, Doc, a boy and a girl." His voice seemed faint, and he rocked back and forth on the stool.

"Well, you can still have more. The other tube is normal, and she has both ovaries."

I thought, *Why would you ever have more after this?*

"I gotta sit down, Doc." Still holding up his gown, the nurse who had led him into the room grabbed Mr. Clark and helped him back out the glass side door into the hallway, where he slammed down on the nearest chair before the door closed.

Sure, I felt wobbly, too, just like Jake. But I just sat down and stared at the floor for a while until Dr. Meyers wanted me to pour ether again.

Mrs. Clark sort of woke up while we were still in the operating room after her bandage was put on. She started to moan and moved around before they tied her to the stretcher. Finally, she answered a couple of questions and sighed when one of the nurses asked her to take a deep breath. I followed along while they carried her back down the stairs to her room. Jake gave Dr. Meyers and my dad bear hugs, and everyone shook hands.

We pulled into that diner on the edge of town for breakfast just as it was getting light. A little bell rang as we opened the door. I was hungry. The only person in there was standing at the sink washing dishes. "Come on in, boys," she said, smiling. "I'm Esther. What'll you have?" She was just a little taller than I was, her face wrinkled except for a strip of bright red lipstick. We sat at the counter on those turning stools I liked.

Esther put her cigarette down on the edge of the stove as she fried our bacon and eggs. About halfway through,

Dad lit another cigarette with his Zippo and leaned across the counter toward me. "Do you have any questions about what happened last night, Bill?"

"Oh, no, Dad. I pretty much understand it all." That's what I said. He had a little smile then. Really, though, I didn't know what had happened, but I wasn't going to show my embarrassing ignorance to him.

But how much blood do we have inside us?

Do other naked women look like that?

That night I learned that people aren't just solid, like trees. They look solid, but you can drip some ether on their faces and reach into them with your hands to fix what's wrong.

Already, at that age, I wanted to be a doctor, especially a surgeon.

***

I remember one unusually stormy Sunday afternoon in December, several years after he had returned from the war; we went hunting together. It was snowing hard; a blizzard covered the roads and fields with heavy snow, and gusty winds blew sheets of snow that stung our faces.

"I see two pheasants above the ditch near the fence," my father said. "I'll drive over the hill and stop. You get out, climb up the ditch, over the fence, and walk back to them. I'll walk back along the road when you reach the farmer's field. We can trap them between us and get them to fly."

I waded through the deep snow in the drifted ditch,

struggled over the sagged barbed wire, and walked back toward the pheasants. One flew up out of range. The other waited and rose slowly into the wind. I shot and he fell into corn stubble. I ran to pick him up, but he was gone, leaving only a small spot of blood in the snow. My right hand was already numb. I decided to walk back to the shelter of trees where I could get out of the blowing storm, pumping out the spent shell casing as I turned. Our old Ford pickup was somewhere far behind. We had smashed through drifted roads, the truck getting pulled and shoved by frozen ruts, the temperature gauge rising into the red until we stopped and dug the snow away from the radiator. No one else had come along the frozen mud road that day.

Why couldn't Dad be like other fathers? Why not play ball, go to a few school open houses? He was so determined, so stubborn. We had stopped playing golf together. If he hit a golf ball off the fairway, he hunted for it until he found it. I used to hunt for the ball too.

"Dad, I found it."

"What brand is it?"

"A Titleist."

"Mine was a Top Flite."

We would continue looking. Other golfers would pass by as we trampled through the woods. Even I, new to the sport, could usually hit a ball straighter on the course and avoid the weeds. He tried to swing each club as hard as possible.

"Slow down your swing, Dad!"

But he was stone deaf to my advice. We spent more

time searching for the correct damn ball than playing golf. I finally avoided that game altogether and took up hunting, but Dad still searched until finding whatever he was looking for, now pheasants instead of golf balls.

"Wait!" he shouted into the wind. "We can track him. See; there's a drop of blood here and another over there; he's going into the short brush along the creek."

Shrouded against the wind, scuffing along after the tracks through the snow, making large ruts up to his knees, he continued the search. I caught up with him as he crouched forward, his snow-covered head and shoulders bent down, scanning for faint tracks. The stinging icy wind brought tears to his eyes—tears that frosted his eyelashes and streaked his cheeks. He carried the shotgun across his chest, right hand near the trigger, barrel on the left shoulder, his bare right index trigger finger coming through a cut slit in his glove, shielded in his palm. Was that the way he had hunted Nazis after Bastogne? We tracked the pheasant through the short prairie grass along the icy frozen creek—just a small drop of blood here and there on brittle weed stems.

"He runs well; you must have just broken a wing," he said. "We'll find him."

The blowing snow covered all the bird's tracks.

"I can't see where he went," I said. "We lost him." My feet were already numb inside snow-caked boots.

"He couldn't have flown with a broken wing. Let's circle carefully. Look before you walk. If you walk over the trail, we'll never find him."

There was a small spot of blood near a fence post.

"He ran along the fence, I guess," I shouted. We kept wading along. The old wire fence, its rusty barbwire mostly hidden beneath the drifts, strung along a small brush-covered hill beside the creek bed we had been following. This was my first time hunting with this shotgun. My parents had given it to me for Christmas a week before. I was ten years old. The 20 gauge could hold five shells, but Dad would only let me have one shell at a time. I was still too young to use the rifle he had sent me from Bastogne for my birthday.

"Make certain the safety is on. Keep your finger on it, and keep the barrel pointed up well away from anyone, and never let dirt or snow get into the barrel. Take the barrel off the gun, and check to make sure it's clear if you have to. Always unload before crossing a fence." After that, he frequently walked in front of me and rarely said another word about the gun.

Suddenly two pheasants flew up in front of us. There was an explosion of snow, loud cackling as the two cocks spiraled upward. I had been looking at the trees and thinking about how it now seemed impossible that I had ever been too warm last summer. How could I have ever gone swimming?

Then came the explosion of snow and the birds jumping up in front of us. My father's gun moved smoothly as he shot twice. Got them both. He picked the birds up, put them into his jacket pouch, and turned, shielding his face from the wind.

"That's the way some things are," he said. "Unexpected. You have to concentrate and plan for what might happen. Let's keep looking for your bird." We circled again and picked up his tracks in the short brush along the creek.

"There he is," I shouted, seeing the feathers against the snow. I ran ahead and picked the dead bird up, placing it in the large pocket in the back of my jacket.

Walking back along the creek, we talked about the hunt. About how good it usually was in snowstorms. Not many hunters, pheasants usually grouped together in cover out of the wind, not running ahead like they often did in good weather—and you could track them easily. We didn't have a dog to help us.

"You just have to be careful to park where you can find your truck in a heavy snowstorm," he continued. "Can't see anything out here—I mean, which direction are we walking? Where did we leave the truck? Can't see the horizon or any buildings. Even the wind is swirling around, so we can't rely on that or even the sun for direction."

"Remember those stories about the pioneers getting lost in the storms?" I said. "I remember one story I read. There was this homesteader who tried to get to the barn to milk his cow during a blizzard. He started out from the house, got mixed up in the storm, and couldn't find the barn. His wife found him frozen stiff the next day."

"Well, that's why you are careful out here on days like this. That's why we parked at the bridge and not just anywhere on the road. We follow the creek; it takes us to the truck."

There was the old red Ford, right by the bridge. We put the birds in the bed of the pickup, unloaded the guns, brushed off our jackets as best we could, and climbed into the cab, clouding the windows with our frosted breath. The engine cranked right up.

"That's another thing about this weather. If you go out like this, you need to know you can get back. You need to take care of your truck—you know, a good battery, lots of gas, tires with good tread. Keep the odds in your favor. What would you have done if the truck hadn't started?"

"Well, I guess I'd just walk along the road until I came to a farmhouse."

"You'd have to be darn lucky," he answered, scraping the frosted windshield with his hand. "I can't see more than a few yards out there. Likely, they'd find you in springtime about when the fence posts melt out of the drifts."

We started off down the road. "Can't turn around because we can't see the edges of the road. Might go in the ditch. I remember this road. It goes for about another mile and then joins a larger north-south gravel road. There's a farmhouse at the corner."

The heater was still blowing cold air as the truck plowed through several small drifts but then slammed into a larger one. Clyde pushed the accelerator down hard, and we plunged forward, the snow flying over the truck. Then everything remained white as the old Ford suddenly stopped. Backward, forward, Dad jammed the shifter back and from reverse to first gear until we smelled burning rubber.

"Damn, we're stuck," he yelled after forcing the snow

away from his opened door and stepping out. "The wheels are lifted off the road with snow jammed under the frame. I know the crossroad and the farmhouse are just a short distance ahead. We'll have to get some help."

I forced my door open and slid waist-deep into the drift we waded through before coming to the more-open road ahead. Soon we could see a faint light to the left.

"There's the farm," I said.

There was no farm dog, no sound of cattle or other animals, no people outside—just wind blasting into the fading dusk and a few lights inside the white clapboard house. A short, stout gray-haired woman, in jeans, a plaid coat, and a red scarf wrapped tightly around her wrinkled head and neck, opened the door after Dad knocked.

"Well, my goodness, look at you two," she said. "Whatever got into you to be out in this awful weather? I've just been out doing feeding and milking chores—had a hard enough time even with that. But you two look half-frozen—come in and get warm. I'll fix you something hot."

"Sorry to bother you. We've been hunting, and our truck got stuck in the heavy snow just a short way down the road to the east," my dad said, pointing to the direction he meant.

"Take your coats off and get warm. Just lean your guns against the corner there." The warm, smoky smell of the roaring fire in the potbelly stove, the sweet, buttery smell from the kitchen—we couldn't resist. "Don't worry about all the snow; it's just a little clean water." My dad removed his cap, and the woman's eyes widened in surprise.

"Why, it's Dr. Meffert. Aren't you Dr. Meffert? You did Harold's surgery. I'm Marge, Marge Wilson. Remember how terrible sick he was that night with his ulcer? He would have died without you, Doc; I'm sure of that."

She raised her hand over her padded coat, about where her stomach would be.

"My, he was in such terrible pain when his ulcer burst. There he was, holding his stomach, reading his last will and testament, making sure all the necessary papers were signed before he let me drive him to the hospital.

"I finally had to grab him and pull him out the door. 'Get the hell into the car!' I said, not proud of it, but that's what it took. Got him down to the hospital; guess it was about midnight, and they called you in for the surgery— remember, Doc? It was last October."

"Well, sure, Marge, of course I remember—had to pull his boots and overalls off him. He wanted us to be sure to give them to you and wanted to know how soon he could go home if he pulled through."

"Harold! Harold! Look who's here. Oh, he's gotten so darn deaf these past years handling all that machinery— just can't get him to see about a hearing aid. He's just in the next room. Harold! Harold!"

He came shuffling through the doorway in his slippers. He had a white, smooth forehead contrasting with a wrinkled, darkly tanned face, shriveled lips holding an unlit cigarette.

"Well, Doc, I'll be goddamned. Thought we were supposed to go to town to see you. Making a house call?"

"Aren't those the same overalls we had to pull off you?"
my dad countered.

"That'd be a fifty-fifty chance, Doc," he said, laughing
as they shook hands. "I'm feeling pretty good now. Not
much pain but tired all the time, and it's been rough as hell
without cigarettes."

"Well, if you don't stop smoking, I may get to operate
on you again, and I'm not looking for more business, so
throw them away. This is my son, Bill."

"Glad to meet ya. Just out looking at the scenery on this
beautiful day?"

"Well, sort of. It's nice out there, really pretty, but the
trouble is our truck is caught in a snowdrift just east of
your house."

"Well, hell, I'll get my coat and boots, fire up the damn
Deere, and pull you out."

"Not until you all have something warm to drink,"
Marge added. "I'll make you turkey sandwiches too. Heaven
knows, we have plenty of leftovers from the holidays. Doc,
does having surgery make you swear all the time?"

"You mean the surgeon or the patient, Marge?" Even I
laughed at that one.

Harold soon got up from the kitchen table. "I'm going
out first. Takes a while to get that old Model A started.
That flywheel will be stiff as hell, and it'll take a while to
put on the front bucket and sweep off the snow." My dad
went out with Harold. I had another sandwich but had
to stop eating when the rough vibrations of the tractor
started, its bright fender lights reflecting off the side of the

house into darkness, as it pushed its way through the snow toward our truck.

I put on the heavy trousers, boots, scarf, and coat, slipping on the wet gloves, and headed for the front door.

"Now, Bill, you come back anytime. Try in the springtime, in good weather—it's so beautiful then—might get Harold to let you drive the tractor! You and your dad be careful driving back!"

I shook her hand and stepped into the snow.

"Here, my gosh, don't forget your gun!" she said, handing me my 20 gauge that I had left leaning in a corner near the front door.

The old tractor pulled the truck out of the drift. Harold had scooped away most of the drift and crawled under the Ford's bumper to put a chain around part of the frame, wrapping the other end around the front of the tractor. As he eased into reverse, the powerful tractor lights showed the drift crumbling as the truck emerged from its white cocoon. We cleaned out the snow from the grille and radiator.

"Let me pay you for this," my dad said.

"Hell no, Doc; you saved my life. What else could compare with that? Just got me out of the house awhile."

"Well, at least take these three pheasants then."

"Ok, Doc. Marge and I really like them. I'll do that. I'll just take one."

"Oh, take all three; then we won't have to clean them when we get home," Dad said.

"Well, all right, I will. Good of you, Doc. You two be

careful out here. Shouldn't be difficult. Just turn south here
at the corner and go until you come to the pavement about
a mile down the road. I heard a plow going south about an
hour ago. You shouldn't have any damn trouble."

"Remember, Harold, no smoking! I would rather see
you here than in the operating room."

"Well, Doc, guess our little encounter that night con-
vinced me. Gum sure as hell is a poor second, though."

The heater finally started working as we drove slowly
home along the highway, listening to the staticky voice of
Jack Benny being broadcast from Palm Springs. *The Lucky
Strike Program.* "In a cigarette, it's the tobacco that counts.
Lucky Strike means fine tobacco—so round, so firm, so
fully packed. LSMFT, LSMFT!" Before the jokes started,
a guy named Don Wilson said something more about
cigarettes:

"Tareyton cigarettes are back. Tareyton cigarettes
were reserved for the armed services, but now the boys are
home and the Tareyton cork tips are back." Then he and
Jack started in, celebrating Mr. Benny's birthday.

My dad reached toward the truck dash, punched in the
lighter, and opened the ashtray. The pungent smell of fresh
tobacco and cigarette smoke filled the cab.

"Good. Always be prepared, Son. That was one hell of a
shot you made today," he said.

"But, Dad, I only got his wing."

He took a big pull on the cigarette. "Hell of a shot. Just
wait until next weekend." He was a better hunter than
golfer.

***

My older cousin, Vince, got a driver's license after the war. His parents had talked with Mom about how teenagers, including Vince, were tearing around in cars now that old cars and gasoline were cheap. They were worried. Then, one night he wrecked an old Ford at two in the morning. His family lived just a few doors down from our home in Iowa. I looked up to him for guidance about acting cool and how to attract girls.

"Don't smile as much. And get away from guys crowding around them—the girls feel trapped and nervous. Relax. When one that's a real babe walks past, you say something like *Great lipstick!* Then, maybe tilt your head a little and just a small grin, not one of your ear-to-ears; but keep lookin' at her, see what she says. It's kinda like fishing for trout."

But after the accident, our parents came down on us both. It seemed to me that all their new rules were like a vise. Vince had to pay for his car's repairs, and since he needed money, he took a job in a nearby grocery store stocking shelves and sent his paychecks to Rod's Auto Repair for the rest of the summer. So he wasn't around much for more of the tips he'd been giving me about how to get the cutest girls to go out on dates.

After the war, I remember telling Dad about breaking up with my first girlfriend. We were walking through a grassy field. He was looking down, trying to find four-leaf clovers, which he thought were omens of good luck.

"Dad," I said, "Cindy and I broke up last week."

"Oh, I hadn't heard about that," he answered, still looking down searching for clovers.

"Well, it feels like I got kicked in the gut; I'm really upset. I've lost my energy. I'm sad."

Dad kept walking slowly, still looking at the ground. He may have smiled slightly.

"No," he said, "your energy and the way you think about life are inside you, part of you, not part of other people. And you are a very strong person."

These few words became fixed in my mind and still are, as if spoken yesterday. I wish I had thanked him then, but he continued walking and, at the time, I didn't realize the power of what he had told me.

I never could see four-leaf clovers while walking, but, during his entire life, whenever the fields were green, he sought their good luck. I suppose many people search for omens of good luck. Perhaps even more avoid what they think might bring bad luck.

I loved even numbers: addresses, lockers, license plates, operating rooms, whatever was even numbered. Odd numbers gave me a vague, uncomfortable unease. When facing stress, especially then, I often looked for even numbers and avoided the odd ones. Like searching for those even-numbered clovers.

***

I hadn't done anything wrong yet, but after the war, when we were all together again, Mom somehow knew fast cars and pretty girls were constantly on my mind. She sensed trouble and decided having me spend the summer in a small sleepy Iowa town was a wise move. One of her relatives, Walt, was a veteran and worked as a carpenter on nearby farms. She called him and offered me at a dollar an hour. I can still hear his deep voice:

"I suppose we could use some help until it starts to snow," Walt said. Then there was a silence like they had disconnected. But then he spoke again.

"Work six days a week. Start at seven in the morning and stop at six in the evening, except Saturdays when I stop at noon, and Sundays when Christine and I go to church and visit with our neighbors." There was another pause, and then he added, "He can stay with us. Plenty of room now with both the kids gone."

"He can stay with us." The words felt like being hit with a sucker punch. I suddenly realized that the exciting weekends, fast cars, dancing, and the parties with smuggled Budweisers I had heard about wouldn't happen for a while. It was like being convicted and sentenced to reform school before the crime had been committed. What could I do? I was innocent.

"Thanks, Walt. We'll have him there next Monday."

"Unless there's a storm," he added. "Then I go to whichever county fair is upwind."

Our family occasionally visited the small town of Van Horne to see my aunt Christine and her husband, Walt. On Sundays, we went with them to the Methodist church on the edge of town. During the sermon, Walt's head would start to nod and then sag onto his chest with ungodly snores followed by laughter from the small congregation. Christine would lift her veil, look at him, and poke his bony chest with an elbow to interrupt his noise. Walt would jerk and wake up for a few minutes, but his snores and the chuckles would resume, only ending when the gray-headed organist played a rousing Christian march in benediction.

I never remembered a thing about the sermons, but Walt became famous, at least in a small Iowa town. I certainly remember him.

Walt was tall, walked crooked and bent like he had hit his head in doorways and now was more careful. He had a nose you could see through in decent light and searching blue eyes deep in his skull, protected by long squinted wrinkles across the sides of his weathered face. Any change of expression came only from his lips. Reddened, sun-damaged hands contrasted with faded, old denim overalls. His farm boots scuffed the floors. He and the other carpenters in his group had already fought in the war, and had been discharged, but I don't remember why.

A sweating, dirt-covered school-kid, I ripped rotten shingles and rusty nails from a deserted barn's roof and slid the sheeting boards down to Walt, who stood on a ladder, with just his eyes and cap visible above the old roof's edge, like peering carefully from a foxhole. The square nails and shingles rained down, and Walt's bare, gnarled hands reached out to grab only the boards sliding past him. He tossed them to the ground below, where other workers sorted the gray, weather-hardened boards, throwing out those broken or splintered and hauling the others up a hill where a new barn was to be built that summer, in 1950.

These were steel-toed, bib-overalled country men; farmers, who had just returned from the war, the killings, and all the close calls. While digging trenches for the new barn foundation, they sometimes would turn up their ruddy faces to watch me tear off the old roof. *They are measuring me,* I thought. They called me "the Kid." Could I work as hard as they worked? Could I keep going despite the heat, or was the Kid just another pussy, like most city teenagers? Late morning, it was hot; the sun bore down like burning metal against my shirtless back that became covered with layers of dirt and old shingle fragments stuck by sweat to my skin.

Finally, it was noon, and I eased down one of the bare rafters and jumped from the roof edge onto a pile of old shingles on the ground, thinking the jump might impress the war veterans. A splintered shingle stuck to my shoe. I pulled it off and walked to a nearby oak tree where we kept our water jugs. Most of the men were sitting there in the shade of the old barn, eating lunch. I sat with them and tried to start a conversation. But they were hard muscled, taut, and carefully quiet. Many of them, including Walt, had lost friends and relatives in the fighting. They sat in the barn shadows, two of them inside one of the doorways. The men ate quickly and almost silently, frequently turning their heads as if cautiously searching for the enemy.

They stayed closely together like hunted animals. I thought about my father, how quiet he was after coming home, and realized that he and these men had not recovered from the war. I wondered how violent they would be if challenged by someone or if their buddies were in danger. Finally, one of the men looked over at me and said, "Hey, Kid, is that a nail sticking out of your shoe?"

I pulled off my work shoe that was stuck by the nail to my foot. It must have been sticking out from the pile of shingles I had jumped on. The nail had buried itself into my foot, and my sock was soaked with blood. Trying to measure up with the other workers, I hadn't felt it.

"You had a tetanus shot?" Walt asked.

"I don't know."

"Just take my old Dodge to Van Horne and get a shot from Doc Dutton," he said, resting against the old barn wall, almost asleep. The farm's two shepherd dogs were napping beside him.

"But I don't have a license."

All the guys laughed. One of them said, "This is Iowa, Kid. And we're in the country. Everyone out here drives when they can reach the pedals."

Getting into Walt's car, I noticed an army rifle and some bullets on the floor of the back seat. I didn't say anything about it to Walt, and drove the gravel to the nearest town, Van Horne, about five miles away. The car's loose steering made it hard to control, and the long ladders strapped to its sides made it difficult to see the road. Most of the way, the wooden-spoked Dodge veered side to side, toward one ditch and then the other, but I finally parked it near a cement wall near Doc's office on Main Street.

Sitting in the waiting room, I thought about that rifle on the floor of the old car. *Mauser* was stamped on the barrel. I had seen them in movies about the war, and Dad had given me one for my birthday just a few years ago. Walt must have brought it home. But why? It seemed too large for game hunting in Iowa. Then they called me into an examining room. The nurse checked my foot and told me to come back if it got sore. After a tetanus shot and a shot of penicillin, I drove back to the farm, skidding back and forth on the roads with clouds of gravel dust trailing behind. I handed the keys to Walt.

"We all had those shots in the army," he said. "I saw one of them tetanus patients in Italy. An Italian soldier had stepped on a piece of shrapnel a week or so earlier. He had been left behind when his buddies retreated. We thought he was laughing at us, and one of my buddies raised his gun to shoot. Then we got closer and saw his whole damn body spasm up when he thought he might get shot. His face was all screwed up—looked like a smile from a distance. We came closer and saw his spasmed muscles caused difficulty in breathing. Several medics strapped him to a stretcher and took the Italian soldier away. One of them looked back at us.

"'That's tetanus,' he said. 'All you guys make sure you got your tetanus shot!'

"But we were more concerned about staying alive fighting the Germans still south of Rome."

At noon the next day, Van Horne's siren blew. We could easily hear it miles away and began walking to the farmhouse for dinner. Walt took me aside to explain that the grandparents of this farm family had once lived in Germany. Their last name was Bauer, and some of them had fought on our side in the war. Before entering their dining room, we washed our faces and brushed our hair with water from a hand pump near the back door. The workers sat with the family at the long table, hesitant to sit at either end, which was thought to be a position of authority. The farmers and the carpenters motioned each other to sit there, and finally the oldest farmer, Karl, sat at one end. The grandmother, who smiled quietly during conversations, sat at the other end, sometimes slipping in German phrases. One of her daughters would then often add "Mama!" There was an uncomfortable silence sitting there looking down the table until Karl finally said the blessing in English with a German accent. We all bowed, held hands, and listened. "God, bless this food on our table. May we use it for the good of others."

"Freiden auf Erden," the grandmother added. A daughter looked up at her mother, but the grandmother raised her hand in defiance and still smiling, whispered, *"Sei ruhig."*

Then huge plates of meat, potatoes, and dishes filled with gravy, applesauce, and loaves of bread were passed. Each of us had separate small plates of cherry Jell-O containing green olives. And pie with ice cream for dessert. I remember the warmth, the feeling of safety, of being accepted and valued most of all.

The army veterans I worked with kept to themselves and helped each other. When it came time to pour the foundation of the new barn, trucks filled with liquid concrete showed up with workers that Walt and his crew didn't know. They were young, muscle-flexing guys not old enough to have fought in the war. Someone called Jake told them what to do. He talked about a new barn Walt had just built on his farm, using boards salvaged from a storm-damaged country school near his farm.

"Ya," Jake said, "they're still talking about them brown and yellow boards mixed with the red ones. Looks like shit!"

Walt's jaw tightened as he moved closer to Jake, but he caught himself. "It suits me fine," he replied, putting his hands back in his pockets while still staring at Jake, who finally turned away.

It was hot and humid that afternoon after a hard rain the previous night. Now there wasn't a cloud in the sky. Because of the slippery mud, the trucks couldn't get up the hill to the trenches for the new barn. Jake turned to his men. "Ok, guys, we'll have to haul the concrete up the hill from the trucks in wheelbarrows. It'll be a hand job." Several of his men chuckled. Walt and our crew watched Jake's men struggle, pushing and pulling the cement-filled wheelbarrows up the hill. Exhausted, one after another broke away to sit in the shade.

"Goddamn," Jake mumbled. "If we don't get it into the trenches in a couple of hours, the concrete will set up in the trucks. Then what the hell will we do?"

We decided to give them a hand, two of us pushing each load of concrete up to the new foundation. None of us said anything. After two hours, sweat dripped from faces and clothing. My hands and arms became slippery and numb, and I was bright red and dizzy. Walt mumbled as our wheelbarrows passed along the hill, "Just another hour of this. Keep drinking, Kid. Just keep drinking. We've got 'em by the balls!"

I kept on pushing the heavy wheelbarrows up the hill until the trucks were emptied of all the cement. By that time, Walt and I plus a few veterans from the war were the only ones left standing. Most of Jake's crew either had gone to see Doc Dutton or were stretched out in the shade of nearby trees. We finished pouring the foundation ourselves. That evening, covered with streaks of dried cement, exhausted and sweat-soaked, I rode with Walt in his old Dodge to his home for a shower and supper. Riding along the gravel roads, watching the scattered farms and large fields of corn and soybeans slide past, I thought about the day's work. Except for Chester, me, and several veterans, the other men had stopped because of fatigue and exhaustion. I had been tougher than most of them, tough as any of them. The old car swerved along on loose gravel; Walt, fighting the steering wheel, looked briefly away from the road and grabbed my shoulder.

"I liked the way you hung in there today," he said.

Staying with Walt and his wife wasn't exactly a bowl of cherries. They both napped after supper, and the radio was full of static. The only magazines I could find had articles about the Miss Iowa contest or talked about farming: like when to plant corn or which tractor was the best. After reading about Miss Iowa and seeing that she lived over a hundred miles away, I looked over his war souvenirs scattered around the living room. Lugers, helmets, swords, gas masks, and several German flags were arranged neatly on tables near the two stuffed chairs they slept in until bedtime. There was a German SS uniform, pressed and protected with plastic, hung in a closet near the front door. Walt woke up and saw me looking at the uniform.

"You ever shot a high-powered rifle?" he asked.

"You mean like the one in your Dodge?" I asked. He nodded.

"After work, I keep it under my bed. Wouldn't be much use in the car with me in bed, would it? Just sleep better with the Mauser close by. It's windy, but still enough light for a little shooting."

He got the gun and a few bullets and met me up in the hayloft of his multicolored barn, where there was a good view of one of his cornfields.

"See that fence post at the edge of the field?" he asked, pointing to a wooden corner post about a quarter mile away. Walt showed me how the gun's bolt action and trigger worked and then inserted a clip of bullets. "Rest the gun on the windowsill and aim about a foot down the post," he said.

I aimed carefully and pulled the trigger. A tremendous

roar and a kick slapped my face. Walt looked at the post and the small cloud of dust to the left of the target.

"You missed it. Didn't 'count for the wind or the long distance. Wind's from the west, so you gotta aim to the west of the post so the bullet will drift east toward the post. Shoot much and you'll get to know about how much to counter the wind." Then he showed me how to adjust for different distances.

"Set it for about four hundred yards."

After a few more shots, I saw a small dark puff of wood rise from the post.

Walt seemed pleased. "Good shot," he said. "You'll get better the more you shoot." Then he turned and looked at me with his arms extended. "God, I hope you never have to shoot anybody. We were in lots of close fighting. Their surprised look, the way they crumple and suddenly fall. Can't get my mind straight. I'll never forget shooting all them soldiers and never forget close friends beside me suddenly disappearing; just a few bloody streaks on the ground and uniform shreds blowing past as we were thinking about going home."

He removed the bullets from the rifle, and we turned to go back to the house. "They weren't someone you knew or hated," he added. "Never met 'em before the shooting started. We were just trying to stay alive and get back home, and so were they. Let the damn politicians fight the next one. Meanwhile, the Mauser stays with me."

It took several months to build that new barn. With school open, I only worked with the carpenters on

Saturdays. The weather started to change. One Saturday in October, strong, cold winds tore at our jackets, and the morning rain became mixed with sleet. The farmers had harvested most of their crops and were loading the new barn with hay while we finished building animal stalls inside the building. By late morning, the noise of tractors and the shouting stopped after all the bales had been hoisted into the hayloft. Still there was a roaring noise outside as strong winds replaced the sounds of harvest. I opened one of the barn doors. It was ripped out of my grasp and slammed against the barn wall. The black sky roiled like boiling tar, and hard sheets of rain pounded down, making it difficult to stand up.

Walt looked up at the storm from the barn doorway. "We should make a break for it," he said, no doubt thinking of a fast drive in his Dodge. But it was too late. Tree limbs, broken lumber, even a child's bicycle flew past us as we stood there, wondering what to do. Just then, we heard the grandmother shout from the farmhouse. *"Komm jetzr her! Komm jetzr her! Schnell! Schnell!"* Karl, slipping and falling, came running out to get us.

"Follow her," he said. "We have a basement."

The farm's two shepherd dogs, the entire German family, and all of us carpenters crammed into the small underground basement. Karl and Chester were able to pull the heavy door closed against strong wind gusts. They latched it, and someone lit a kerosene lamp. We were standing crowded together, worried about ourselves and each other in that gray light with the sounds of screaming wind and loose boards slamming against the house. The dogs whined and made their rounds to each of us as if checking to see if we were all present. The grandmother looked up at the cellar door, clasped her hands, and shouted, *"Gott bewahre uns, Gott bewahre uns."*

My father must have heard those same words in Germany with Patton's army. For years after returning home from Germany, he attended his army hospital's reunions and must have talked about experiences with other army doctors, especially after treating so many wounded soldiers from both sides during the Battle of the Bulge. But he never talked with me much about his war experiences.

***

On weekends, I left the farm and my work with Walt and got rides back to my parents' home, twenty miles away. I sat through church services with my mother on Sunday mornings. I listened to the sermons, but most of all, I could hear a cute young girl roller-skating and laughing in the church basement. Her name was Mimi. We were both in the same junior school. I had known about her for a couple of years. She was energetic, smart, and always seemed to be having a good time, but she was much too young for me.

IOWA (1950s)

Of course, I dated in high school and even went steady a few times with several other girls, but, after being dropped from the basketball team (when I threw the ball at the hoop, it usually bounced off the backboard), most of my extracurricular time was devoted to wrestling. That sport required hours of conditioning and participation in wrestling challenges in order to make the varsity team before matches with other teams. I was strong for my size and quick moving. My father had also wrestled in college. Our build and size were similar. I worked hard and practiced almost every night. Eventually, after a year or so, I won almost all my matches and decided to enter the Iowa state wrestling tournament. My mother had developed a routine of fixing a light meal of toast and honey and tea for me just after weigh-in, and then I would take a short nap. Then she would wake me up and drive me to the match. My dad almost always came to the home matches, and once in a while to tournaments when they were out of town. He was usually late. I often saw him open the door to the gym just before my match. He would sit quietly in one of the upper rows. The season was long, and we frequently travelled for matches to other cities and tournaments. Weight control was necessary to pass the weigh-in before the matches. I either wrestled in a weight class heavier than I normally weighed or had to lose five or six pounds to make a lower weight class.

I remember one of the district matches to qualify for the state tournament against an excellent team from Davenport. My mom and dad came into the auditorium, late as usual; they sat quite far from the wrestling mats. I was at least a point behind for most of that match. The crowd was mostly cheering for my opponent, who was stronger but not as quick. Finally, only fifteen seconds remained in the match. I was exhausted but caught him a little unbalanced and swung under his arm, threw him down on the mat, and scored two points immediately before the final buzzer, winning by just one point. There was lots of cheering because it had been a very close match, but there were also some boos. The medals were awarded immediately after each match. I took my medal up into the audience to Mom and Dad. Later, when I got home, Dad had already gone to bed, but Mom was still in our kitchen with a meal for me. We sat at the kitchen table.

"Bill, that was quite a match! We were sitting near people who cheered and yelled loudly for your opponent. Dad got angry with their shouts. I tried to calm him down, but finally he stood up, turned around, raised his fists, and shouted back at them, 'You shut up! That's my son fighting the boy you're cheering for!'"

I was surprised and pleased that Dad was willing to risk a fight to support me. We shook hands when I took the medal to Mom and Dad in the bleachers. There was no more booing.

Sometimes, at home after the matches, Dad and I would discuss techniques and the advantages of certain moves and certain holds, but I never learned much about the sport from him. Just the drive and the determination. Break something if you must, but don't ever give up. After eight years of high school and college wrestling, I had plenty of damage: most of my front teeth were chipped from opponents' heads hitting my jaw, and several other teeth had been lost after damage to their nerves. Also, a cauliflower ear, and eventually a hip and two shoulder replacements later in life. My mother and her sisters thought the injuries were horrible, but I was pleased to finally be good at something.

"Why do you do that?" they would say. "Why not tennis or track? You are a fast runner."

But to Dad, these injuries were part of wrestling, part of learning never to give up, and wrestling gave me determination and self-respect.

***

The most important thing to me about that match Mom and I were talking about was that both sides had cheerleaders, and this young girl, Mimi, was cheering for our team and for me! She was the girl whom I had heard rollerskating during our church service. Wearing a short white skirt, bright red lipstick, and a cabled white sweater, she shook pom-poms and leaped high into the air, cheering for our team. Then she looked at me, pointed a pom, and smiled. For me, our age difference suddenly seemed less important. Perhaps it was even desirable. She had become such an athlete! Later that night after the wrestling match, we met again at the A&W Root Beer drive-in. It wasn't a date, really. We were in separate cars that were parked side by side; the cheerleaders in one, some beat-up wrestlers in the other. We talked back and forth, smiled, and laughed a lot. She seemed so happy, like a breath of fresh air. For me, that was the beginning of a love still present after sixty-five years. Did I mention she was homecoming queen in high school? I loved everything about her.

COLLEGE AND MEDICAL SCHOOL YEARS

We were far apart during college. I drove my Ford from Duke to see Mimi at Ohio Wesleyan; she flew to North Carolina several times, usually for our Joe College Weekends. I remember how she loved dancing to Les Brown's jazz during those weekends. We talked about the future sometimes, but even after dating for two years, the future seemed so distant that we drifted apart. I phoned to ask her to Joe College Weekend again when I was a senior.

She replied, "I'll have to think about it, Bill." There was silence. The silence of indecision. (She had started to date some guy in her class at Ohio Wesleyan who ended up a urologist in Cincinnati.)

"Well, let me know what you plan to do," I answered. "Joe College is only three weeks away, and I'll need to get a date soon if you decide not to come."

I thought the distance between us and our infrequent visits had finally been too much. I loved her and thought she loved me also, but several years of letters were no substitute for being together. Neither one of us said goodbye on the phone. Neither one of us was to blame. Thinking our love was hopeless, I didn't write letters to her or try to call her. I wasn't going to try to sell myself to her and couldn't go to visit her without some sort of encouragement or invitation. A week passed without a phone call or a letter, so I asked Marge, a cute girl in my chemistry class, for a date to the weekend party. She agreed to go with me.

A day or two later, Mimi called me and said she'd like to come to Joe College Weekend. I told her I already had a date. There was long-distance silence.

"But I'll see if I can rearrange things," I finally said.

Gloomy clouds suddenly cleared to bright sunshine. But now I had two dates for Joe College! I'm not proud of what I did then. Marge had already agreed to go with me that weekend. I called Marge in her Duke dormitory.

"Marge, thanks for agreeing on our date," I said.

"I'm really looking forward to being with you for Joe College," she answered.

Mouth dry, I stared at the floor of the phone booth. I couldn't tell her about Mimi's phone call. I couldn't think of what to say.

"My mother's having a serious operation. That's what I'm calling about," I finally replied in a higher than usual voice. "I think I should go back to Iowa to be with her." I felt like a rat, a desperate rat.

"And stay there for at least a week," I added. "I'll have to miss Joe College."

Silence.

"I think family comes first," she added. Her voice was without its usual sweetness. "I'm sorry, but you are doing the right thing." Then she hung up.

Marge was a quick-thinking, smart girl. It was obvious

that she saw through the excuse. She was hurt and angry, just as I would have been.

Mimi arrived on the Friday night before the big weekend. She stepped from the airplane wearing a snappy red dress that matched her lipstick. She smiled. I waved. We saw each other and moved through the crowded room until we touched. We embraced, mindless of others around us. The next afternoon, Les Brown played jazz in a large grassy university quad crowded with students sitting on blankets. We sat close to the band surrounded by fraternity brothers and their dates. It was a cloudless, pleasant afternoon. We shared our picnic lunch and talked about the future more than we listened to Les Brown. Her perfume was intoxicating.

I hadn't told Mimi about Marge. I was tense. What if someone found out about my double cross?

Then Mimi said, "Let's go see your roommate play lacrosse."

My roommate, Don, was an All-American on the Duke team that was playing at home that day. It was just a short walk to the lacrosse field. We arrived after the game was about half over; the bleachers were almost full, and the crowd was shouting and cheering. Shocked, I saw Marge with some other girls sitting up high in the audience. She was without a date.

"I don't see any seats," I said.

"There are two just in front of those girls near the top," Mimi said, and started up the aisle. Each step brought us closer to Marge, who had stopped shouting and stared at both of us. Mimi sat down quickly in one of the available seats just in front of Marge. I sat quietly beside Mimi, my backside uncomfortably hot and vulnerable. Mimi cheered when my roommate made points. I sat there like a post. It had been a cruel deception, and I had been caught. I should have handled things differently, perhaps faking a sudden illness or getting a fraternity brother to put one of my arms in a cast. But Marge was sharp. She would have easily seen through those schemes. We never talked to each other after that day, and I didn't blame her.

Perhaps I should have told Mimi I had a date already and tried to get together with her on another weekend. That might have been the best choice. But I had never met anyone else with such a comforting lightness and persistent optimism. I wanted to be with her, to marry her. Being together on this weekend might be our last chance to renew our thoughts and hopes; to renew our love for each other. Joe College Weekend, the loud celebrations, the music and dancing, might help Mimi and me to think less about the uncertainties and separations in our future and just reach out and enjoy each other. It might be our last chance.

During my first two years of medical school, my old Ford coupe put on lots more miles and needed several sets of tires. New Haven, Connecticut, and Delaware, Ohio, were a long way apart even above the speed limits. She flew to New York and met me several times each year for long weekends together.

Her parents wanted Mimi to wait for marriage at least until she had graduated from college. Then, one night when she was visiting, she mentioned she had decided to graduate from college in three years instead of four. Both of us were shocked that we might be able to end our separation one year earlier than we had planned.

She was twenty-one and I was twenty-four when we married. Neither of us had finished our education. She earned a master's degree in history at Yale. I completed a six-year surgical residency at the same university. It must have been from her that our three children inherited a steady, pragmatic optimism and great physical abilities. I thought I had gone to heaven.

When I was a first-year resident in surgery, my parents came to visit us in New Haven. One night when I was on duty in the hospital, the page operator asked me to call her. Telling me about a family emergency, she sounded anxious and sad while giving me a number to call. It was Mom:

"Bill, I think Clyde is having a heart attack. We are back at the hotel. He's having chest pain and is pale and sweaty."

"Oh, Mom, I'm so sorry. I'll be right there. Call for an ambulance." Another resident covered me while I raced to the hotel.

Dad was as pale as the sheets covering him. He was sweaty; his radial pulse was weak, thready, and rapid. Almost silent; his distant unblinking stare reminded me of patients I had seen near death. No need for a blood pressure cuff. The medics arrived just a few minutes later. In the emergency room, the EKG showed electrical changes consistent with a large heart attack. Over the next hours, his appearance improved, but the enzymes showed that significant damage had occurred to the back of his heart. He was anticoagulated and kept on bed rest for three weeks by the cardiologists. No coronary angiography or angioplasties were then available. The mortality for such a large heart attack was 30 percent. But he did well and joked with the cardiologists during his recovery. Then he and I flew back to Iowa. We sat in our seats before takeoff. He turned to me with a smile.

"Well, that was an interesting experience. The doctors say no cigarettes and no work for another month. And Dr. Goodyear said it would be a good idea to take a drink of Scotch in the evenings."

"Do it, Dad. Just do it." It was the first time I had thought about his health, his eventual death. Probably the first time I had given him serious advice—a dictum.

He cut down on smoking and stopped travelling to small out-of-town hospitals for night emergencies. Several of his friends had died from severe heart attacks. He knew he had been fortunate to survive. It must have been difficult, but he accepted my advice. But I worried about his health. I knew because he had suffered a large heart attack in his sixties, his chances of surviving ten years without more additional heart problems or even death were slim.

VIETNAM (1968–1969)

The Vietnam War raged while I was in training. It had been a cruel myth that World War I—or any war that followed—was the wars to end all wars. Would there ever be any peace on Earth? I worried that even our son would fight in some future war. The army was desperate for doctors, especially for surgeons. My wife and I realized that most young surgeons would be drafted. I volunteered to enter the army if the army would allow me to finish my six years of surgical residency first. By that time, I had completed four years of college, four years of medical school, and six years of surgical residency and was almost thirty years old. The length of army duty was two to three years with options to sign up for additional years and possible future promotions. Physicians who had finished training were drafted into the army as captains and promoted to the rank of major after one year, assuming their performance in the army was satisfactory.

We hadn't yet left New Haven when orders for Vietnam arrived. I had seen newsclips from Vietnam; the large numbers of wounded, the dangerous, heroic medevac evacuations of critically wounded soldiers. Multiple severe wounds, avulsed arms and legs, and massive bleeding were things I had rarely encountered in training. I felt inadequate and too inexperienced to treat those injuries. The thought of being in a combat zone for a year was frightening. What if I were crippled or killed like the soldiers I had seen in videos? I had never before contemplated that. What would Mimi and our children, Stephen and Mollie, do? I hadn't yet started a career after years of training. Mimi and I decided to move back to Iowa and wait for further orders. We had both grown up there, and our two sets of parents lived there. It would be a good and safe place for our children. We phoned our parents about my orders, and Mimi asked if she and our children could stay with them until I returned from Vietnam. At the time, it seemed to me almost like a gift to our parents to have Mimi, our son Stephen, now eight, and Mollie, four, stay with them. All four grandparents immediately said yes. But I had over-looked all the inconveniences, the noises, the runny noses, and the time our parents would spend reading and talking with our children. All the important things that I, thinking about the war, had just assumed they each would find time for in their busy schedules. It was a lot to ask, and today I realize it was rude, impolite, and even disrespectful. I even asked my father if he could teach our children about na-ture by showing them his love of the outdoors, and show them how to find four-leaf clovers. No parent said no to any request or added any conditions.

I called my dad. "Dad, I don't think I know enough to take care of wounded soldiers. We have been trained to operate with preoperative information from blood tests and mul-tiple X-rays. Careful, precise operative techniques don't seem a good fit to treat wounds I have seen from the war videos." There was silence, a pause. Then he answered.

"Years ago when I finished my training, my chief said, 'You haven't seen every problem yet, and I'm certain you never will. But you are well trained and intelligent. You will have to think on your feet; you'll have to improvise.'" Another pause for a few seconds and then he continued. "Know your anatomy; stop the bleeding; and then think of the ways to repair the damaged organs. Stay in control and think rapidly. No one can treat that soldier better than you."

My father insisted I take his .32 pistol he had carried in Patton's army.

"Just use it if you are very close to the enemy," he said.

We practiced shooting that gun into a deserted riverbank. It became too hot to hold. I couldn't imagine using it to shoot someone, but I knew how to do it.

"Use wire to close wounds," my father said.

I had used silk and synthetic sutures in residency. Did he really think I would use silk in infected wounds? We didn't argue, but, in Vietnam, I used synthetic sutures that also resisted infections and tied more easily than wire. Their only disadvantage was a tendency for the knot to slip after it was tied. That could cause an intended wound closure to loosen. Fortunately, the synthetic sutures were easily tied with one hand, and adding one or two more knot layers while tying these sutures solved that problem.

> San Antonio, Texas
> August 25, 1968
> Fort Sam Houston
>
> Dear Mimi and family,
> Thanks for the reminder to keep my backside down this next week. Actually I hadn't planned to wave it in the air or waste any time crawling across a field under machine gun fire. We will have two evasion

problems involving taking a few of us at a time out someplace with a compass to see if we can find our way back to Camp Bullis without "enemy patrols" capturing us. Later next week, we will study American aid stations and hospitals that simulate those in Vietnam, and practice unloading casualties from helicopters, ambulances, and armored personnel carriers. Then we will operate on sheep that have been shot with M16s and see how much damage to soft tissues and bones is caused by high-velocity bullets. Finally, for fun on Friday, we will be gassed with tear gas while wearing gas masks. All the time getting paid by the army!

It seems years since I have seen and touched you, sweetheart. And yes, I do dream about you.

I love you, Bill

ON THE WAY TO WAR (1968)

I tucked the .32 into my boot before getting on the plane to Saigon.

We left Travis Air Force Base at midnight. Two hundred soldiers, straight faced, silent, wearing fatigues, and carrying M16s. Uncreased fresh faces, just beginning to shave their upper lips. I felt like their father. Could I stop their bleeding? Was I ready? How many would die? I watched the lights of San Francisco disappear behind the wing. Would any of us see those lights again? While flying over the Pacific Ocean in the darkness of early morning, the constant roar of jet engines and the crowded, uncomfortable seating somehow made it easier to think about the past than future unknowns. What would happen to Mimi and the children if I didn't return? Mimi had a master's degree in history from Yale. She could teach, but we had no reserve funds, and she would not want to depend further on our parents, who had contributed for years to our educations.

I thought about the mistake of leaving New Haven without thanking the many people for their years of help in medical school and during my years of surgical training. But at that time, focusing on my orders for Vietnam, with the dangers and unknowns, had crowded out the good judgment of maintaining previous friendships. I spent time with the family, sorted books, made lists of performed operations, journals, clothing, telephone numbers, letters, and addresses that I needed to have with me during the next year. I hoped to be able to prepare for surgical board examinations while in Vietnam.

I thought about the Saturday picnic our family was invited to just before I left for Vietnam. The party had been in the park of Van Horne, that small Iowa town my mother had sent me to for several summers to work with Walt when I was in high school. Many aunts and uncles, including Walt, who taught me how to build barns, came with their families and brought food and drinks. The baseball game, kids' swings, teeter-totters, the merry-go-rounds—it was their way of saying goodbye, good luck. But, thoughtless at the time, I took it as just a fun gathering of relatives, not them saying goodbye and good luck to me. I didn't realize the picnic had been for me until I was no longer in Iowa. Again, I had not said many thank-yous. I should have stood up on a chair or table and expressed my thanks to all when they gathered together after the picnic. Now, on the way to Vietnam, it was too late.

Aside from the picnic, many friends and relatives came to my parents' home when I was there, sorting through lists of personal and professional things I hoped to take with me to Vietnam. I know their visits were intended to express concerns about my safety and to talk about our good times of the past and how we'd have more when I returned.

But at times, those visits reminded me of visits to the terminally ill, when relatives and friends relate happy past events, and give their thanks to the poorly responsive person stretched out in bed; only I was still standing. Family and friends often show more kindness and spend more time with the person prior to their death than when they were in good health. After leaving a visit to an ill person and walking back to their car, someone might volunteer, "God, he looked terrible—so pale, so fragile. It won't be long now."

I wondered what they had said about me.

"Pale, quiet, confused, stiff uniform, looked scared."

"Well, wouldn't you be scared shitless too? Let's get back

home. Got chores to do before Cronkite comes on. Maybe there'll be some good news for a change."

The departing person had been excessively thanked but had not properly thanked people for their friendships and their concerns. I hoped for a chance to do a better job of it when I returned. I had a lot to learn about taking care of others besides their physical needs, and a lot to teach our children about maintaining friendships.

***

Where would I be in Vietnam? What type of surgery would I perform? I had been well trained and owed my family and my professors for their efforts and sacrifices. It was payback time, whatever happened. I was going to be there for a year and resolved to do my best to help as many soldiers as possible. But I had heard about the lack of security, the ambushes, and booby traps, and the isolated shootings in what were thought to be safe areas. We had not been briefed about the exact kinds of possible enemy attacks, their weapons, or even what precautions we should take. I suppose the type and intensity of fighting and the necessary precautions would depend on where we were stationed; none of us on the airplane had specific orders.

We refueled in Honolulu and Guam. Jets filled with GIs returning from Vietnam had already landed there. All the soldiers mixed together—ecstatic, drunk soldiers who had survived and depressed, frightened soldiers on their way to war.

"Keep your heads down, motherfuckers. Remember, your M16 rifle is your ticket home; keep the damn thing clean. You couldn't pay me enough to spend another year in Nam. I was lucky. Maybe you will be too!"

I couldn't relax with all the shouting and celebrations. I had to return to the john to take a leak after they left the airport.

At sunup, I looked ahead and saw the greenness of Vietnam. We spiraled down steeply to avoid enemy fire and landed at the Ben Hoa Air Base crowded with Phantom and Super Sabre fighters landing with their braking parachutes deployed, and others taking off with bombs suspended beneath their wings like egg-bearing insects. The aircraft doors opened. Hot, humid air poured into the jet. We walked off the 707's ramp onto the tarmac; the steaming black asphalt stuck to our boots. The humid air smelled of kerosene and rotten jungle. A thermometer in the large arrival tent beside an aircraft hangar registered 104 degrees.

We formed a line and listened to a sergeant. "Those of you leaving for the north will fly out tomorrow afternoon. There are cots in the next tent for sleeping tonight. We get frequent rocket attacks at night plus occasional sappers trying to blow up buildings and planes."

He paused to wipe sweat from his face.

"If you hear explosions, sirens, or gunfire, don't just lie there in your beds. Run like hell to those sandbagged bunkers near the mess hall. Someone will come and get you when the party's over. Last week we lost two new guys who stayed in bed when their tent caught a direct rocket hit."

The sergeant's deeply sunburned face was lined with sweat dripping from his metal glasses and soaking his fatigues. He paused, looked directly at all of us, in Vietnam for less than an hour.

"This is something you can tell your grandkids about," he said.

I just wanted to survive and to *have* grandkids.

DA NANG (1968–1969)

The next day, I joined several other GIs with orders for Da Nang. We crowded into a four-engine C-130 cargo plane and sat on long canvas benches among Vietnamese soldiers armed with M16s, ammunition clips, and strings of loosely hung grenades attached to their belts. Their placid, small wives and children sat nearby. Wandering chickens and pigs filled spaces on the aircraft floor. The air smelled of rotting vegetation, pissing pigs, and mud-caked people smoking Vietnamese cigarettes. My thoughts were on rifles casually pointed at me from across the aisle, dangling hand grenades with delicate safety pins, and knives carried by Asians whose faces I had no experience reading.

When I arrived at the Da Nang army hospital, it was dark. Nearby villages smelled of rotten fish and burning charcoal. I met George, the thoracic surgeon I was to replace. Thin, sandy-haired, and hollow-eyed, he was bent over a table examining a pistol-trigger assembly with two other doctors, all of them cleaning pistols and discussing the week's problem cases. George left Vietnam two days later. It had been a calm period, those two days. I hoped it would continue.

Da Nang; September 15, 1968

> Dear Mimi and family,
> Arrived at the evacuation hospital in Da Nang. Flew from Saigon to Da Nang two days ago in the hold of a boiling hot C-130 cargo plane. For some of us it was standing room only. Vietnamese soldiers and their wives crowded together, smoking, laughing, swinging rifles around with hand grenades hanging loosely from their belts. Children, chickens, and pigs squeezed between our legs. I was the least armed on the plane with Dad's .32 pistol tucked in my right boot.
> Anyway, we made it.
> Love you all, Bill

Iowa; October 1968

> Dear Bill,
> So wonderful to get your address and first letter and to finally know where you are. I told Steve you were in Vietnam and wouldn't be home for a few months. He looked up at me and hugged my knees.

"Well, Mommy, we will just pretend that he had to go to the hospital for a long operation." Hard to hold the tears. More later. Need to put the kids to bed.

Love forever, Mimi

***

This is what I remember about those first months: It was a hot summer. I stood on the beach staring at a battleship firing heavy shells whistling over our army hospital, exploding somewhere beyond the Da Nang airport miles away. I flicked away blood flecks from my hands, rubbing them gently in the sand. Flakes of dried blood fell from my face; blood clots clung to my scrubs and fastened several toes to the primitive sandals strapped to my feet. Like a scary clown in some horror movie. I spit sand into a sink and breathed odors of decay and antiseptics. I no longer wore fatigues or boots, just shorts and T shirts, sweat-soaked and smeared with soldiers' blood. I drank from a water canteen while jiggling blood clots were scooped from floors with shovels. Helicopters landed; dozens of fresh casualties suddenly appeared. Medics ran to the admissions ward with blood bags and additional dressings. Patients were rushed to surgery. I never imagined it would be such utter chaos.

Then it suddenly became quiet and calm. We played volleyball and slept. Lou Cincinotta broke his foot playing volleyball. The lucky stiff was evacuated, smiling all the way to Hawaii, I suppose. We all wanted to break a foot. Tape recorders played "The Green, Green Grass of Home" and "All You Need Is Love." One entire day without performing surgery. That had not happened before. It might have been the first war when you could be killed listening to your favorite songs.

A burly hospital supply sergeant worked closely with a young Vietnamese woman who organized equipment and uniforms for new arrivals. A hot affair quickly developed. He asked our urologist to urgently perform a vasectomy before more fighting occurred.

"Well, I don't know," the doctor replied. "It's probably against some regulation, probably illegal."

"We can skip all the paperwork," the sergeant replied. "Just use a little local anesthesia. Could even do it in the supply building, after hours."

"Oh, I don't know. It sounds so unethical."

A pause in the conversation.

"Would the doctors like a jeep of their own for a few months?"

Another pause.

"Ok, I'll do it."

Later in the day, the sergeant got his vasectomy in the supply department office. The following week, a new jeep appeared. The sergeant healed as if nothing had happened.

Things went along smoothly for a few months. We often drove the jeep to nearby American marine bases and a navy hospital because their food was so much better. They served fresh red meat.

Then, one day, a jeep with fender flags came roaring up to the hospital. The driver and a colonel's supply officer talked quietly with our vasectomized sergeant, who waited for them at the hospital entrance. Our jeep disappeared. The new number we had painted on the jeep's bumper just happened to be the same as the colonel's.

***

Then days of chaos again. Chinook helicopters landed on the beach near the hospital. I held my breath and covered my eyes as kerosene fumes and sheets of sand blew through the hospital. Wounded soldiers were carried on stretchers into Admissions, a drab, open-ended Quonset Hut, painted with red crosses.

One soldier had suffered a brain injury, a traumatic amputation of one leg, and a severe abdominal injury. We took him to surgery first. After two hours and twenty transfusions, he became seriously hypothermic. His blood no longer clotted; he suffered a cardiac arrest and could not be revived. I was exhausted, dehydrated, and depressed. A canteen of water seemed too heavy to lift. Why had I ever become a surgeon? Any other specialty, but not surgery.

I could imagine that soldier's mother praying. Kneeling, hands folded, head bowed, pleading for his safe return, as she had done each day since he left home. He was removed from the table and replaced by a curly-haired kid from Iowa with a belly wound and fractured legs. I began the surgery; blood spilled out of his abdomen through the incision, splashing everyone before pooling on the floor. His liver was fractured, but somehow the bullet missed the aorta and the vena cava. I removed most of the right lobe of the liver, which was a dull gray instead of a normal red color. The bleeding stopped. My sweat dripped into the wound. He survived.

I tried to remember some of the names or the injuries of the soldiers I operated on, but I could not. There were so many.

***

Father Perez remembered, though. He was the Catholic priest. He went from soldier to wounded soldier, comforting, taking down names, giving last rites, laying on his hands. He was always there in the hospital, even when rockets hit nearby. He wore sagging fatigues, and sweated like everyone else, with a bottle of tequila in one pocket and holy water in another. His vestment was a long green stole draped over his wet shirt and doubled back over a shoulder when he knelt at the soldiers' sides. I stared at him, trying to read what the hell was printed on his stole, probably Latin, a language I had disliked ever since being tortured by a high school Latin teacher, Miss Turner, whom I was certain had never had sex and probably would have even turned down Julius Caesar.

Perhaps Perez actually believed in the spirit, life after death. Well, he could have that belief. The dead looked dead to me.

He gave last rites to the living. But I saw him give last rites to the dead too. I reminded him of the difference between life and death. He held up his hands. "You don't always know," he said.

Midnight. I heard a truck. A canvas-backed military truck was parking beside the admissions ward. A rocket had struck a nearby orphanage. Perez was already there. The canvas was thrown back, uncovering a mound of silent children. Arms, legs, bodies mixed together, bound with blood that dripped from the truck. We sorted the children. The dead were kept together; those alive or possibly alive were put on stretchers. I looked at the mangled bodies with Perez as he gave last rites. One child, a small boy, cried. I saw he had no legs. One arm was missing, and so was his other hand. Tears mixed with my sweat.

"He is alive! He lives!" Perez said. "He has a soul! We must try to save him."

For what? I thought. *He will beg and slowly starve. He has no family; there is no one to help him.*

Perez continued. "He has a soul! Who are we to judge about what we do not know?" He looked at me with reddened eyes, his hand on my shoulder. "There are no funerals or flowers. We do what we can."

Damn Perez and his religious principles. I took the boy to surgery, and he somehow survived. As days passed, I stopped to see him; now a sort of human pillow propped by stuffed toys and carefully cared for by nurses. I looked at him and was worried. He smiled at me. I was depressed. What had I done?

As a medical student, I recited the Hippocratic oath. Innocent, even ignorant, I held my hand high. *First, do no harm,* it read. So simple when problems are distant. But what if all choices are bad, even catastrophic? No one else understood the problems we faced when dozens of critically wounded were suddenly brought to us by helicopters. Then we almost always operated without other physicians similarly trained. When we were making surgical decisions, no one was available to give advice. We were totally alone.

There is a moment when the wounded progress from pleading for help to the silence of accepting death. I'm trying to remember now, but except for his crying, I think the boy was silent. Perhaps he was in shock; maybe he couldn't speak. Maybe he couldn't find any words.

That night, I would have rather been Father Perez.

Da Nang; November 11, 1968

> Dear Dad,
>
> Slightly cooler now, but still in shorts and T-shirts and still sweat soaked all day long. We have been busy with the steady arrival of seriously wounded during the past week. I'm getting more efficient, which is fortunate because I often see injuries I've never encountered before and have to figure out what to do in the operating room.
>
> Small incision, small surgeon—I've

heard that in training as a sort of joke. However, with these injuries, I've found, unless the patient is in extremis, it's best not to commit to an initial incision any larger than necessary to discover which organs are damaged and then enlarge or change the incision if necessary for repair of the damage. Many other wounded soldiers are waiting for surgery, so I try to keep moving along.

A Vietnamese surgeon, Dr. Phouc, visited our hospital last week. He asked if we could help them at the civilian hospital, which is across Da Nang, near the airport. I plan to go there next week to see the hospital and meet other doctors who work there.

I suppose the fall colors are beautiful now and pheasant season is open. I miss spending time with you especially this time of year. I'll still enjoy hunting even after this! Take care of yourself and Mom.

Love, Bill

Iowa; November 28, 1968

Bill,

Driving through Da Nang to the Vietnamese hospital doesn't sound like a good idea to me. You sent some photographs recently. I think they were taken on top of Monkey Mountain or from some other hill near the hospital.

Why don't you just stay closer to your hospital? Isn't it dangerous to be running around? Sounds to me that there is plenty to do at the hospital. If you get tired of the routine, read a book, study for your boards, or take a nap. You have responsibilities here at home, you know.

Love, Dad

Da Nang; December 1968

Dad,

Thanks for your last letter. I understand your concerns about driving through Da Nang to work at Vietnamese hospitals. Even so, we are being very careful. I remember you writing about taking walks away from your hospital when you were in Czechoslovakia, and how you felt safer with your German shepherd than walking alone through the nearby forests. It must have been a relief to get away from all the war wounds, even just for a few hours. I feel the same relief when taking care of civilians and the many surgical problems they have, not related to the fighting.

We have begun transferring some

Mom and William, 1943

Dr. Clyde Meffert, 109th Evacuation Hospital, Czechoslovakia, 1944

William, Stephen, and Mimi, Iowa, 1964

Dr. William Meffert, 95th Evacuation Hospital, Da Nang, Vietnam, 1968

Standing on the site of the former 95th Evacuation Hospital

Stephen, William, and
Dr. Dung, Da Nang, 2020

Remains of Khe Sanh trenches, Vietnam

Remains of Khe Sanh trenches, Vietnam

Dr. William Meffert and the grandson of an NVA
soldier killed during the battle for Khe Sanh

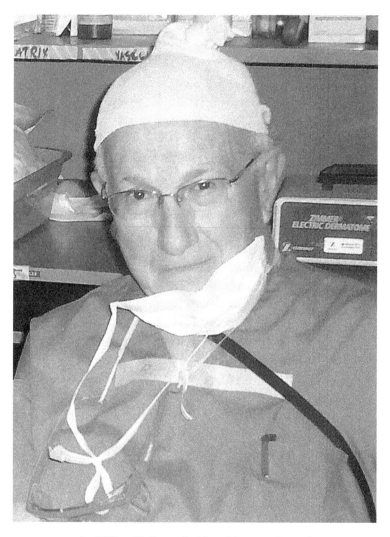

Dr. William Meffert at the Albert Schweitzer Hospital

civilians with complicated problems to our army hospital and keeping them in tents near the admissions ward. More pre-op tests are available in our hospital than in the Vietnamese hospitals, and also, like the military patients at our hospital, civilians are carefully treated medically and may receive surgery when lulls in the fighting occur. Now, most of our visits to Vietnamese hospitals are to choose patients for transfers.

Take care of yourself, Dad. Get enough rest.

Love, Bill

I knew he realized the dangers of driving a jeep through a crowded, unsecure city like Da Nang. I never wrote about the thrown hand grenades and the occasional shootings of Americans. This was a war that brought no security to soldiers on either side. Unlike most previous wars, there were no battle lines, just series of ambushes, patrols, firebases, taking and giving back hills, body counts, and propaganda from both sides, each claiming they were winning.

We took care of many Viet Cong patients in civilian and Vietnamese army hospitals and hoped that this might make attacks on hospitals less likely. Operating on civilians with surgical problems unrelated to war such as hernias, perforated stomach ulcers, and newborn abnormalities helped balance the stresses of combat surgery. To me, the work in the Vietnamese hospitals was worth the risk. I carried an M16, a .45 pistol, and wore a flak vest and a steel helmet when we drove through Da Nang; the jeep driver, an American soldier, guarded the parked jeep until we returned to our army hospital.

***

Three a.m.

"Major, we have casualties, sir." A corpsman stood beside my cot.

"Ok, ok." I stumbled over my AK-47, the flak vest, and the helmet laid out on the floor each night, fumbled into my cutoff fatigues and T-shirt, slipped on thongs, and started running along the beach toward the admissions ward. The helicopters had already gone. Those damn ocean breakers—never heard a thing. Most casualties, like this night, arrived at our hospital in the late afternoon or during the night, when ambushes were more difficult to avoid. Fading sunlight and dense shade along jungle trails made trip wires and partially concealed spikes or pungi stakes more difficult to see. Hidden explosives included grenades that sprung up in the air several feet before exploding. Helping a wounded soldier would often bring additional mortar, grenade, and rifle fire.

Twelve wounded Vietnamese lay on stretchers with the fetid smell of blood, feces, and the stink of helicopter kerosene—the perfume of combat trauma. Some were partially covered by blood-soaked clothing draped over exposed bowel; others had limbs hanging precariously from plundered bodies, and some lay quietly with head injuries. Other wounded were wild and screamed wide-eyed at the medics who rapidly removed shoes, cut off clothes, and started intravenous fluids.

I looked at a young Vietnamese man with sharply cut bleeding wounds scattered along his left side and a larger, deeper wound low in his chest. Probably injured from a hidden Bouncing Betty grenade fired by a trip wire strung across a jungle trail and covered with leaves. No breath sounds could be heard in his left chest. His breathing was labored; his blood pressure was low, but his abdomen was soft and felt normal.

Air and blood shot out under pressure when a tube was inserted into the chest and connected to suction. The man's breathing eased. But the chest X-ray showed a chunk of metal low in his left chest against the spine, near the aorta and esophagus.

I remembered a Vietnamese soldier a month before with a similar wound involving the esophagus. He had been rushed into the admissions ward in shock, injured by a bullet entering the left chest and exiting low from the right chest wall. A trembling, tearful, shoeless boy, his son, clutched the stretcher and never lifted his gaze as his father was taken to surgery. The boy's expression of fright and sorrow became fixed in my mind, like a repeating recording. It started before his father's surgery and now, fifty years later, I still see the boy holding the stretcher, not talking, staring at his father's head, but not appearing to see through his tears.

I had opened that soldier's left chest, sutured several bleeding arteries, and hurriedly closed a hole in the esophagus as the patient's blood pressure drifted downward. I had guessed wrong: serious bleeding continued from behind the heart into the other chest near the exit wound where the liver dome had been shattered. The patient was turned and another incision made. Clots and liquid blood were everywhere—spilling off the table and splashing onto the floor, soaking our feet. The bleeding had finally been controlled with gauze packing firmly inserted into the liver's tears.

That night became a recurrent tipping point for me; the Vietnamese boy's face—sometimes crying, sometimes shouting angry, unknown words, but usually just unreadable as he sat staring silently on the floor under his father's stretcher. Just waiting.

At first, that soldier had done well, but he gradually began to run a persistent fever. As days passed, the gauze pack was slowly removed without further bleeding from the patient's liver, but he showed signs of infection, probably from breakdown of the esophageal repair. We were too busy with fresh casualties to investigate, and the patient became too ill to tolerate another major operation. He just gradually slipped away. We tried not to frighten the boy, whose silent eyes followed us each day. When his father died, the boy disappeared. No one, not even Tram Thi, the female interpreter, knew what had happened to him. Visions of the boy and his father's blood returned to me each night, finally dimmed by additional, more recent tragedies. However, even now, years later, I see the boy's face, his eyes; I understand his silent prayers that went un-answered. I would have given anything to have saved his father.

I was determined not to have the same result with this patient. His left chest was painted with iodine and draped with sterile green sheets. I cut into the chest cavity, re-tracted the lung, and saw the black menacing chunk of shrapnel, which had torn the esophagus just above the dia-phragm and then slammed into the vertebral column, nar-rowly missing the aorta. Bubbles of air and green mucus oozed out of the esophageal rent. The patient was stable; there was minimal bleeding, and the operating team re-laxed. The team was ready to start the surgery.

"Princess" was the surgical nurse's nickname. The Princess crowded against me to get a view into the wound. Our heads would sometimes collide. Her perfume wasn't bad, just a little jarring in a combat zone. But her dangling left earring kept banging against my ear as she handed me the correct instruments. No one spoke much. The face of that boy, who had stayed under his father's stretcher a few weeks previously, floated across my vision; part of a collage of bloody images. I repaired the wound in the esophagus, but this time opened the diaphragm and pulled up a small part of the stomach to suture over the damaged esophagus. After removing the chunk of shrapnel, I carefully irrigated the chest cavity with sterile saline and closed the chest after leaving a tube for temporary drainage.

I looked up at the anesthesiologist, who always wore a

towel wrapped around his bald head during surgery. How could he be cold? I called him "the Sultan." We often operated together at night. He called me "the Night Rider."

"Sult, this time I'm going to keep all fluids away from the injury."

A tube was placed into the stomach through a small incision in the abdomen to drain secretions out of the stomach. Another tube was placed into the small intestine to feed the patient while healing progressed. A third tube was placed into the upper esophagus through a small neck incision to drain saliva and keep the repair dry.

"I'll pull all these tubes out in a couple of weeks after making sure the repair is intact."

"Sure, sure, Rider, whatever you say—let's get out of here and back to sleep."

The man was taken to the intensive care unit. Over the next few days, he did well as feeding progressed through the small bowel tube and the other tubes drained his secretions. Walking for the frail man was difficult even with help from his family. His paper slippers scraped along the hospital floors, and the fragile hospital gown slipped off his shoulders even when snapped tightly. He had obviously lost weight, but no fever was present. The patient seemed comfortable but very quiet. He spoke no English, and I spoke very little Vietnamese. "Pham" was the name on his armband. He may have been VC; some Chinese grenades were found near him—it didn't really matter to me. I scheduled an X-ray for the following day to study the repair before removing the tubes. They came to take him for the study, but the patient was gone; the hospital was searched without finding him. I finally found Tram Thi, the interpreter.

"Where's Pham?" I asked her. She looked frightened.

"He take big swim in ocean during the night!"

"But I was going to take the tubes out later today," I answered. "He could have lived a normal life."

The interpreter's mouth opened as she raised her hand to cover it. Her eyes became huge and rounded.

"Oh! He not know that! He say he not live with tubes!"

Da Nang; January 29, 1969

> Stephen and Mollie,
>
> Stephen, I should tell you that Dr. Phouc picked out a tiger's claw for you one day last week when we went shopping together in downtown Da Nang. He insisted on getting it for you. Perhaps after it arrives, you could write him a thank-you note. Just send it to me and I'll give it to him. Thanks, Dad.
>
> Mollie, how is your swimming coming? Are you and Steve becoming experts? In just a few weeks, I hope to see you in Hawaii and watch you two swim in the ocean.
>
> Love, Dad

The family seemed so far away. Without looking at their photographs, I had difficulty visualizing the children's faces and even Mimi's. That worried me; I wanted to stay close to them in my thoughts, to effortlessly see them in my mind. It helped to know they were safe and loved in Iowa. I could separate them from my life in a combat zone. There were two separate lives for me, and I had strong family love and support. Even so, my letters to them seemed stilted and unnatural, like I was writing to people I hardly knew.

Vietnamese doctors visited our four-hundred-bed army hospital frequently; they included Dr. Phouc, a Vietnamese surgeon whose training had been interrupted by the war. After we examined patients together for several mornings, he asked me to visit the Vietnamese civilian hospital. I had heard that hospital also had hundreds of patients but lacked the ability to care for seriously wounded patients. I decided to accept his invitation to visit.

One early morning the next week, a sergeant checked out a jeep from the nearby motor pool after showing the supply officer a copy of our orders. We threw in our duffel bags, put on flak vests, strapped on helmets, loaded our M16s and .45 pistols, and holstered several grenades after checking that the safety pins were securely in place. The road near the airport was almost free of traffic, but then nearing the bridge over the Han River, there were crowds of people heading to the downtown market. Some led pigs or carried caged songbirds. Chickens, their legs tied together, hung silently draped over shoulders, only their heads moving. Other people pulled heavy carts filled with blackened bowls of rice, fish, or vegetables. Bloody hands carried dripping, raw, unwrapped meat. Motor scooters, double ridden, wove between bicycles and pedicabs even at seven in the morning. Most Vietnamese looked down or just a short distance ahead, their thoughts hidden behind expressionless faces beneath large pointed *nón lá* hats kept tightly strapped to their chins. The carts, heading to market, were often loosely covered with dark canvas, and this early in the day, many people wore loose jackets and trousers. I kept my M16 at the ready with my finger on the safety near the trigger and turned to Mel, who was driving.

"Shit, Mel, stay away from those crowds. I can't see what they're carrying. Might be a grenade or even an AK rifle."

We inched across the bridge, where marines in full battle gear guarded the unloading of supply ships. A short distance closer to the ocean, a German hospital ship, the *Helgoland*, was anchored in the river against the west bank and painted a bright white. Its wide gangplank was crowded with Vietnamese patients coming and going. I had heard that many Viet Cong soldiers dressed in civilian clothes infiltrated the city and received treatment there.

I turned to Mel. "How can it be painted such a bright color in a war zone? Everything else is drab-colored or camouflaged. There aren't even soldiers guarding the ship."

"Well, Germany's not fighting this war, and the ship's probably a sanctuary for the VC and whoever else goes there for treatment. No questions asked."

Vietnamese working at our hospital said the *Helgoland* was safe when it was docked in the Han River; mortar and satchel charge attacks seldom occurred then. We knew the ship managed to sail out to sea just in time to escape attacks in downtown Da Nang. They must have had inside information not shared with us.

"I heard the Germans don't even check IDs," Mel added.

"Sons of bitches, they must reason it buys protection; that it's worthwhile even though it harms us eventually."

But I realized that we, too, operated on VC soldiers and probably some of their families. At night, there were guards around our hospital, but they usually worked in the hospital and were not combat trained. The enemy must have valued having us nearby and did not directly attack our compound.

After crossing the bridge, we headed north. The narrow asphalt road was crowded with military trucks, armored personnel carriers, jeeps, and motorcycles. Though it was still early morning, it was summertime and the air was already hot, humid, and heavily fouled with exhaust fumes. After a few miles, there was a sign for the Vietnamese hospital, pointing to a small sandy road near the Han River. We drove past a dismal shack where the road curved away from the river. A small shattered glass window hung from its frame, and a dirt-streaked sheet covered the front doorway. The roof, held up by several posts, was missing shingles and partly collapsed. An old white-haired, bearded papasan sat on the porch. His eyes followed us with a disgusted look on his face, as if thinking, *First the Chinese, then the French, then the Japanese, now the Americans.* He raised a hand and pointed to the doorway behind him, shouting, "Suckie, fuckie."

Mel turned to me. "I'm desperate, but not that desperate."

"Must'a been the corner that made you slow down."

The disgusted look of the papasan . . . He might as well have been shouting at us, *Any foreigners who assume they can control us are not only unwelcome; they will fail.* And the worst part—if someone tried to help or invade us in America, I would probably feel the same way as the papasan. Mel interrupted my thoughts.

"Last week, someone walked past our jeep in the Vietnamese hospital parking lot and put a grenade under a wheel. One of our soldiers was watching the parking lot and caught the bastard. I'll stay near the jeep while you're inside the hospital."

Dr. Phouc met me at the hospital entrance. We stepped over broken stones and pieces of fallen plaster littering the entrance. Inside, the gray walls were smeared and stained with old blood and body fluids. The dark, unlit hallways were crowded with people sitting on the floor. Many were wounded with fresh injuries and covered with bright blood. Others, unbandaged with infected wounds, lay waiting for someone, anyone, to help them. Several soldiers lay against a wall, their eyes and mouths widely opened; they didn't move as we walked past them. Dr. Phouc, his eyes magnified by wire-rimmed glasses, was quiet and straight lipped as we turned to enter the emergency room. "We'll cut through here to the stairs. You ok?" Phouc asked.

It was hot. The foul air smelled of rot and infection. Sweat ran down my face and stained my fatigues. I felt nauseated and not just from the heat.

"I'm doing fine," I answered. Dr. Phouc walked ahead of me through the emergency room. The wounded were crowded together on shelves stacked three and four high against one wall; others lay on the floor. Patients with burns mixed with amputees; several soldiers with belly or chest wounds shouted and cried for help. Open wounds were covered with flies. Those with head injuries were quiet except for their moans. Several nurses were on duty, but there were no doctors. *If there is a hell, it can't be any worse than this,* I thought. I stopped and took a drink from my canteen.

It would be much better to be killed fighting in the jungle. Before today, the injured soldiers I had seen were rapidly flown from the jungle to our evacuation hospital. I had never seen so many uncared-for patients gathered together, injured in so many different places in so many different ways.

We stepped carefully to the stairway and walked up to the second floor; many of the glass windows were missing in the long, narrow surgical ward. A thin layer of smoke hung against the ceiling. Looking down, I could see people crowded around ground fires in a small, dingy courtyard. Large blackened pots filled with boiling water and vegetables sat on the open fires between the hospital and another building Phouc said was filled with patients suffering from tuberculosis.

Several hundred patients crowded the surgical ward; two long rows of ancient beds crowded each other and pushed against peeling yellow walls. Bandaged Vietnamese filled a littered center aisle. Forty sheetless beds, eighty patients—a forest of heads and eyes followed us as we walked slowly, stopping to examine the war wounds and to discuss details of management. Infected wounds drained down patients' sides; tubes drained air and pus from chest wounds into half-filled Coke bottles. Many wounds were uncovered. There were no sterile dressings, no running water, and no way for anyone to wash hands.

Phouc told me an American professor had recently visited the hospital and *demanded* to wash his hands. The next day, there was a faucet on the wall with the miracle of running water. The professor had been impressed, according to Phouc, but two days later, the flow suddenly stopped. The professor had curiously opened the closet behind the faucet and found a small barrel of water on a table with a pipe running from the barrel through the wall to the faucet. There was a drowned rat in the barrel, its head jammed into the pipe entrance. Lots of jokes about that—Dr. Phouc took the rat's side:

"Just think. He must have smelled the water from a long distance and crawled into the closet, up the barrel, had a drink, gone for a nice swim, and then been sucked into the pipe when the professor washed his hands."

I noted that the barrel had "Water" printed on the side. "Well, Phouc, there's the problem—he was an educated rat—could read English. 'Water, Do Not Enter' would have been safer."

Phouc countered with a slight smile. "It might have been safer not to know English!"

We continued walking along the hall, examining patients with old wounds who had somehow managed to survive and partially heal without surgery. A thin, wrinkled old man with a long scar on his neck had a tube draining from his left chest into a Coke bottle. A crowd of patients watched with us as he drank some orange Kool-Aid, which immediately came out the chest tube into the bottle. Having performed this trick dozens of times, he smiled and bowed, stroking his beard as other patients pointed at the tube and bottle, shouting and clapping with surprise and laughter. Another man, younger, probably a soldier at one time, smiled and pointed to a purple, softball-sized pulsating mass just below his left clavicle. Expanding and contracting with each heartbeat, the thinly stretched skin looked ready to burst. A young girl had a gunshot-damaged carotid artery filled with clots; some of the clots had broken loose and lodged in her brain. She struggled unsuccessfully to greet the doctors while her left hand and left leg dangled off the bed.

Many of these injuries would have been fatal if inflicted from a slightly different direction. Survival was measured in millimeters. Lucky or unlucky? Dr. Phouc then led me up another shattered stairway to the third floor, where more civilians were hospitalized. Several patients had severe heart failure from leaking or narrowed heart valves after suffering rheumatic fever. I listened with my stethoscope to what I thought were soft blowing sounds of blood flowing through narrow openings and loud snaps of thickened valve leaflets. The diagnosis of mitral stenosis was probably correct, but I needed a quieter room to be certain. We walked slowly along the aisle. Patients who could still walk or limp lined up behind us, holding up their shirts or rearranging clothing to point to their injuries, a medical Pied Piper parade. I had never seen so many patients pleading for help. The Vietnamese doctors were overwhelmed. There was no order of treatment, no schedule, no plans even for the next day.

"We operate on these patients when we can, when the fighting tapers off, and there aren't many fresh casualties," Phouc continued with his soft, musical accent. "Many more patients with serious surgical problems are in the Vietnamese army hospital across town. We only have room for a few here, where the families provide food and most of the care until we can get to them."

My back and chest were soaked; sweat dripped off my chin. I could feel it run down my chest and abdomen, past my crotch to my knees. Dr. Phouc had broad wet streaks on his shirt and trousers. He gazed down again at black-clad women in the dark courtyard, still bent over steaming sooted pots; sweat dripped from his metal-rimmed glasses.

Dr. Phouc and I began operating together at the Vietnamese hospitals whenever we could during lapses in the fighting. First, less complicated wounds were repaired, but then after a few weeks, a woman with a destroyed tuberculous left lung was selected for surgery and taken to the ancient, dingy operating room. Surgery was progressing smoothly with the left chest open and the lung exposed when we both noticed the patient's blood becoming very dark; there was intense talking in Vietnamese at the head of the table. The breathing tube had fallen out of the patient's mouth onto the floor. Dr. Phouc stepped to the head of the table behind the drapes and spoke a few loud words to the anesthetist. There was movement at the table head. The blood became normally colored, and Phouc returned to the patient's side.

"Whatever you said seemed to help, Phouc."

"I told them to use some fucking tape to fasten the tube to the patient's face and to be more careful!"

Just then, the blood became dark again, and Phouc stepped to the head of the table, his voice louder and more persistent as he repeated the same words. I looked over the drape at the anesthesiologist. "God bless adhesive tape!" Nobody laughed. We finally finished the operation but after that decided to take Vietnamese patients with complicated wounds to the American evacuation hospital.

***

A large tent was constructed beside our army hospital where civilians with unrepaired, complicated vascular and chest wounds crowded on narrow cots alongside other

Vietnamese patients with heart failure following rheumatic fever.

Dr. Phouc rode to our hospital on his motorbike. Sometimes his wife, Hai Anh, sitting sidesaddle on the rear of the motorbike, came with him. Her face reflected the slim, graceful effects of French and Vietnamese heritage. She was also a doctor, but compared to us, floated gracefully along in her *ao dai* (a long-sleeved, usually ankle-length tunic worn over trousers) while making rounds. We performed careful physical examinations, ordered a few laboratory tests, discussed surgical strategy and risks, and selected patients facing grim futures without surgery.

One day after working together to remove a damaged leg artery that threatened to burst and replacing it with a Dacron tube, Phouc looked at me while I was writing postoperative orders in the intensive care unit.

"What can be done to help patients with scarred mitral valves and heart failure like the young women we examined two weeks ago at the civilian hospital? Have you ever operated on the heart?"

"Never alone, just helped professors," I replied. "We used heart-lung machines to stop the heart for an accurate, open repair. We had lots of expert help."

"But these people will live only one or two more years with severe heart failure," Hai Anh replied. "Isn't there a technique that breaks open the narrow valve by placing a finger in the left atrium and forcing the valve open?"

I thought about my residency training. Operating on a heart while it was actively pumping blood had been completely displaced by heart-lung machines. The new techniques allowed stopping the heart, evacuating the blood it contained, and opening the quiet heart to repair cardiac valves with excellent visibility.

"I've never seen a surgeon insert a finger into the beating heart to break open the mitral valve. Just read about it and heard old professors talk about the unpredictable results. Either the valve couldn't be forced open with finger pressure because of heavy scarring and calcium deposits, or it would suddenly split open too far."

I stopped writing postop orders and looked at Phouc. "Sometimes calcium dislodged from the stiff heart valves during that surgery and embolized to the brain, causing strokes. Our hospital X-ray machines are not sensitive enough to show calcium in the heart."

"What's wrong with trying?" Phouc replied. "We could open the left chest, put a finger into the heart through a purse-string suture, and feel the valve. Too much calcium or too stiff a valve and we'd just pull out the finger and close the heart."

"I've never liked surgical situations that offer only one way in and one way out—no way to escape from serious complications. What if the valve is calcified? What is too much—a dangerous amount—and what is an acceptable amount?"

"Then they will all die," Dr. Phouc replied. "I have seen them become desperately short of breath, clinging to beds, forcing air in and out, unable to eat, swelling with fluid until they lose strength and—"

"Phouc, you know losing a patient during elective surgery is different from losing a seriously wounded patient on the operating table. It's a death we directly cause—one that didn't have to happen that day."

"Of course," Phouc answered. "We see death every day—even sometimes causing it ourselves. At least we try to save them. We can't always be correct, can't always take the right path. God will watch over us and give us strength."

I was impressed with his empathy and his willingness to try even old, obsolete procedures while trying to save his patients. I finished writing orders and glanced quietly around the busy intensive care ward, finally looking at Phouc and Hai Anh.

"One of my professors used to say, 'Don't try to screw the unscrewable.'"

We were silent then, but, after having repaired hundreds of severe military wounds, I realized that performing more elective surgery, even cardiac surgery, in a combat zone might preserve a measure of sanity for us; besides, the patients we had examined in severe heart failure had no future without repair of their scarred heart valves.

We were young then, young and perhaps not yet tamed by postoperative surgical problems sometimes associated with aggressive or risky surgical procedures. Our judgment may have also been influenced by the despair of daily confronting severe injuries and death. I was not aware that any other army hospital in a combat zone had performed heart operations in Vietnam or during previous wars.

Hopefully the screw was not unscrewable.

Quy Lien had been brought to the civilian hospital by her family. She was unable to work, short of breath even while walking slowly, wheezing except when resting; a persistent cough interrupted her sleep. She was a tiny young woman, her conical hat pulled tightly and a white *ao dai* split at the waist revealing her black trousers and swollen feet indented by sandals.

Dr. Phouc translated. "Her mother says she has been sick for over a year and unable to work in the rice fields. Her legs became large a few months ago, and now she can't breathe."

The patient lay down on a stretcher, looking up at us like a helpless, trapped animal; muscle-wasted and wheezing, her heart raced with a blowing murmur and the leaflet snap of mitral stenosis. She could not survive long with so little blood pumped through her narrowed mitral valve.

I reviewed the anatomy of the heart and the normal pressures inside its chambers with Dr. Phouc and Dr. Hai Anh. It seemed to be a relatively simple operation. The most critical part was selecting patients without modern techniques such as cardiac catheterization to measure pressures in the heart chambers and to be certain that the clinical diagnosis of the valve dysfunction was correct. Fortunately, an excellent cardiologist, Dr. Politte, was also stationed at our hospital. His experience in listening to abnormal hearts enabled him to accurately select potential surgical patients by quietly listening to their hearts.

Perhaps the risk of calcium tearing the heart wall or breaking away from the surgical site could be minimized by selecting only young patients who would have had fewer years to calcify their valves.

With rest, digitalis, and diuretics, Quy slowly improved and was then taken to surgery. Her left chest was opened to expose the sac around the heart. The sac was opened, and a purse-string suture was placed on the left atrium. I inserted an index finger through the purse string into the left atrium. The high pressure in the atrium surprised me. Like a narrowed drain prevents water from emptying a sink, the blood was prevented from flowing normally through the narrow valve. My finger was drawn down to the mitral valve by rapidly flowing blood. The valve would admit only a fingertip. The patient's entire cardiac output of blood rushed through the pencil-sized opening. A finger placed into the narrowed valve completely shut off the flow of blood to her left ventricle and to her body. Her blood pressure plummeted until I pulled my finger back up into her left atrium. The valve felt firm but without any calcium. I removed my finger from the purse string.

"Feel this," I said. Phouc, with a wide-eyed expression, inserted his finger into the atrium. "Feel the valve?" I asked. "Feel the opening and the scar that fuses the leaflets?"

Phouc's startled eyes enlarged as he explored the heart's interior. "Shall we split it open?" He removed his finger. She was tolerating surgery well.

I again inserted my index finger into the patient's left atrium and slowly extended it to force open the valve. It only opened slightly. Then I pushed firmly in the other direction with a flexed finger. The fused leaflets suddenly split apart. Now the first and second fingers together slid through the opened valve. Concerned the split had been excessive; I withdrew my finger into the atrium, above the valve. Fortunately, no backward flow of blood through the valve was present. I had never seen or performed this operation before. Even so, now the valve functioned well.

Quy recovered rapidly. Her heart now pumped blood normally. A few days after surgery, Dr. Politte listened to her heart with his stethoscope and smiled. The pathologic murmur of the valve had disappeared. As days passed, she lost most of the excess fluid that had distorted her body. She began to look emaciated rather than puffy. Now that she was no longer short of breath, her huge appetite brought strength and energy. She soon was helping other civilians waiting in the tent for a lull in the fighting.

Later, in January, with a background of mortar and artillery fire, we sat in the intensive care unit after successfully operating on four more cardiac patients. The fading light shadowed and partially hid Phouc's tired face as he looked up from the gray concrete floor, past the rows of white-cocooned patients, and stared at his wife.

"I hear a murmur when I listen to my mother's heart," Dr. Hai Anh said. "She can't walk without gasping. I think she has mitral stenosis like the other patients we have operated on. Would you consider fixing the problem? I'm afraid without your help she will soon die."

Dr. Phouc and Hai Anh brought her frail mother to the American hospital in an army ambulance despite the increasing tempo of combat and the flow of wounded to the hospital. She walked slowly in her white *ao dai* into the admissions ward, stopping several times to breathe deeply. The heart murmur was similar to the other patients', but she was decades older and more likely to have calcium in her damaged valve. During surgery, knife-like spicules of calcium could cut through the cardiac wall or embolize to other parts of her body.

"Surgery is her only chance," Hai Anh said. "My family prays for us at their shrine. It is risky but the only chance she has."

During the next few days, the fighting became intense west of Da Nang toward the Ho Chi Minh Trail, with heavy nightlong artillery fire and the thudding shake of detonating bombs. The battleship *New Jersey* moved closer to the shore and began firing, the heavy shells screaming past our hospital without warning. Helicopters filled with wounded landed all day and night for the next week, filling the admissions ward and covering part of the landing pad with wounded and dead soldiers.

An ammunition dump near the Han River exploded, hurling blackened chunks of metal over the city and near the hospital. Nearby, enemy rocket hits sent dirt raining down from ceilings into open wounds, and at times the lights went out. Operating teams wore helmets and flak vests underneath sterile gowns and operated with flashlights.

The tent beside the hospital emptied. The Vietnamese patients and their families left for safer shelter. Hai Anh's parents had gone with the others. No trace remained of anyone who had waited there so patiently, and Dr. Phouc no longer rode the motorbike with his wife along the edge of the South China Sea.

Da Nang; February 16, 1969

Dad,

Heavy casualties lately, both day and night. No time for elective surgery. It makes me wonder about our government's plan to win the war by pacification. Many casualties come from retaking hills and valleys we previously have occupied. Generals talk about favorable body counts and winning the hearts of villagers. I think unless people feel safe, they won't be loyal to either side. Without eliminating the inflow of fresh enemy troops, this doesn't seem possible to me.

Yesterday I operated on a Vietnamese officer with a severe abdominal injury. I closed many bowel perforations, resected part of his stomach and pancreas, and removed his spleen. Today, I saw him pushing his IV pole down the hall with his young son. Tough people!

Take care and get enough rest, Dad.

Love, Bill

***

The morgue was on the left of the corridor leading to our sleeping quarters. The morgue doors were wide open, with cots closely spaced on each side of a narrow central aisle. Friend or foe, Americans or Vietnamese. They were together, some staring at the ceiling, others missing body parts or unrecognizable. It was the place men went if they had been unlucky or unwise. So many injuries successfully treated in the operating rooms had just missed vital arteries and veins or had damaged but not divided these vital vessels. During surgery, I had often wondered how the injured soldiers could have been so fortunate. A fragment of a grenade or bullet had just missed the aorta or the vena cava or the spinal cord. The injuries had been serious, but many vital organs had been spared.

The morgue told the rest of the story and revealed the entire truth. Those soldiers' last letters probably hadn't yet reached home. Their families didn't yet know they had been killed. There was no grieving. Just bodies to ship out in the morning. We felt lucky and guilty to be alive. Those poor damn soldiers.

I looked at my roommate Graham, a surgeon whom I greatly respected and had, at times, operated with. We sat on a bench, crumpled against a wall, just outside of the operating rooms, waiting a few minutes while the rooms were cleaned. Both of us had been operating through the night. Orderlies again scooped blood from the surgical floors with shovels, pushing the jiggling clots into large plastic bags for incineration.

Graham: face wrinkled past his age, a cigarette dangling, eyes closed, blood on his tank top and shorts, dried clots on his feet and sandals.

"I never imagined it would be like this," he said, recalling how it had been those first days in Vietnam, well-trained, eager, and inexperienced. Back then, we saluted, dressed in fatigues and boots instead of shorts, and attended the bullshit staff meetings and participated in inspections by colonels and a few passing generals. Even went to church every Sunday, with the comforting belief that God's providence would give us guidance. *Onward, Christian soldiers.*

A few minutes later, two twin-rotor Chinook helicopters landed beside the hospital on the beach of the South China Sea. We held our breath and covered our eyes as kerosene fumes and sheets of sand blew through the flimsy buildings. Twenty casualties were unloaded and carried on stretchers into Admissions. Graham ground out his cigarette. We both stood up to make room as patients were wheeled rapidly along the narrow corridor into the operating rooms. A curly-haired kid with a belly wound was placed on the table in operating room number one and rapidly anesthetized. Graham began the operation; blood spilled out of the abdomen through the incision, splashing everyone before pooling on the floor. Somehow the bullet had missed the aorta and the vena cava by millimeters.

I walked over to Admissions to examine more of the wounded. A soldier was sitting on the edge of a stretcher, a strip of white skull showing from a bullet wound to his head. He talked about an ambush and thanked God, while someone cleaned off caked blood from his face and hair.

I looked at the skull that was fortunately still intact, but there wasn't enough scalp to cover the bone. I gently grasped the soldier's arm. The soldier silently looked up at me, as if expecting solace. But I was lost, thinking about how to move his scalp. I had never seen a similar injury. Where should I make the incisions? The scalp would have to be pulled from behind his ears to cover the exposed skull. I thought skin grafts would be necessary to close the open wounds behind the soldier's ears. Father Perez, the Catholic chaplain, knelt briefly beside the wounded man, holding his hand and offering prayers before the soldier was taken to surgery.

"Frenchie and I were sitting there in the jungle, opening some rations for dinner," the soldier said. "I bent forward to open one of the cans on the ground just as the bullet grazed the back of my head and then hit poor Frenchie in the chest. I know he's dead. I saw you guys cover him up after we got out of the helicopter. He was bad in the air, could hardly talk, but kept asking if I was ok.

"What the hell am I going to tell his parents? I mean, we were friends. We grew up together." He bent forward, holding his head with bloody hands.

"I tried to stop the bleeding. I held my hands against his chest, stuffed some of his shirt into the opening. But the blood kept running along the helicopter floor and out the open door. Oh my God."

Pale tears tracked across his scuffed face. "What will I tell his parents? Oh my God!"

Father Perez knelt beside the wounded man, holding his hand and offering prayers. He talked softly to the patient. "I'll help you write a letter to Frenchie's family," he said. Then Father resumed giving last rites to dying soldiers and blessing the dead. The admissions ward was restocked, put back on alert, the blood scooped away.

Late in the afternoon, on the way back to our hooch, we again walked past the morgue. Frenchie was lying there with all the other dead bodies and piles of human parts. A moment too soon or too late, an inch this way or that, it seemed that it was just chance if you did or didn't end up staring at the morgue ceiling, toe-tagged like Frenchie.

This war was different from Dad's. There were no battle lines, also no real security, no safe zones, and no relaxing. In the beginning, I had thought God was watching and would protect the *just* side, but after a few months in the combat zone, life or death seemed just chance. Besides, was there a *just* side? There were villains and heroes on both sides.

It was a coin flip whether a soldier turned or bent over or straightened up at the same fraction of a second when a sniper pulled the trigger. Whether you stepped on an undisturbed trail or stepped on a concealed mortar shell buried beneath a layer of leaves on the trail made all the difference. Life or death. How would you be warned? And the enemy rockets. They were not accurate. The enemy was not trying to kill you; they just wanted to destroy your fire-base, your company headquarters, or your airplane.

"Sorry, GI. We could have been friends in a few years. So sorry."

And there was no security for the enemy either. Anyone out at night, anyone wearing black, anyone who ran through the paddy fields—they were the enemy. They were part of the body count.

I thought about Dad taking care of the German soldiers. I think he took pity on their beat-up condition. They were taken care of like our soldiers in his hospital. I felt the same way as he did. These soldiers, from both sides, were fighting for the same things: to safely go to work and return to their homes and their families; for security of their loved ones; and freedom from self-interested politicians who sent soldiers to settle disagreements, or even to die, for their often-obscene ideals. All of us from each army could have justifiably fought together against this unfairness.

I remember my father returning from the war, not talking much, perhaps because of his anger at political leaders who had caused the sacrifice of millions of people. He was not angry at the Germans or the German soldiers; just at their leaders and their demands of genocide to "purify" the German race. A few years after the war, he bought a new car: a Volkswagen!

After the war, I never saw him go to bed before kneeling at his bedside. I wish I had asked him what he prayed about. I wanted to know what he was thinking. Probably thanking God for his survival and asking forgiveness for being unable to save so many seriously wounded soldiers. He was a deeply religious person who was very private about his beliefs.

He rarely made it to church except for Christmas and Easter. I remember one Easter Sunday; Dad shook hands with the preacher after the service. "I don't make it here very often," he said, "but I thought you gave a thoughtful sermon."

"If you can't attend, then you're just too busy," the preacher replied.

I thought the preacher was an ignorant, thankless person. His remark to my father showed his lack of knowledge of the hundreds of lives my father had saved. He didn't understand that the soldiers who fought while he was at home in his protected pulpit might have saved his life and the lives of his family.

I was so thankful that Mimi, our children, and our families were safe and away from this war that was destroying everything in its path like an evil tornado spreading across hundreds of miles. I prayed that our seven-year-old son, Steve, would not be involved in this or other endless wars. What actually were we doing here? What just cause were we fighting for? Serious injury or loss of a family member in this or a similar war would be heartbreaking.

After months of taking care of many wounded from both sides and reading about favorable body counts in the army's newspaper, *Stars and Stripes*, it was difficult not to become depressed and angry. Wounded Vietnamese civilian patients often told interpreters in our hospital that the Vietnamese government didn't care about people living in the countryside who were forced to move from their old hamlets, their family gravesites, and their farmland.

Those living in these small hamlets were often herded by the government into new, "more defendable" hamlets, their land and previous villages destroyed, all of their possessions including livestock left behind. Their weapons for defense were often taken by the enemy, who recruited new members from Vietnamese farmers, angry because unwise policies had taken away their homes and their villages. The local VC often helped farmers plant and harvest rice. They provided minor medical and surgical care and even taught classes. They wisely blended into the rest of the rural population. It seemed to me that this war was a stalemate without end.

*＊＊

That evening, a monsoon storm swept over Da Nang. White-crested waves crashed onto the beach, sending blasts of water and sand into our hooch. We tried to rest before the usual night combat began. I covered my mouth and nose with a thin blanket. Graham stood up and tilted his narrow canvas cot, showering the floor with sand before flicking the ash-tipped cigarette away and lying down again on his side of the plywood room.

"Maybe the rain will keep everyone under cover, and tonight we'll be able to get up a game of poker," he said.

Dried blood clots lay on the floor near his cot and still clung to the bottom of his sandals.

"We've got to get Perez in a game again," I answered. "That stone face of his. He hides his weak cards. Hell, I'm down a month's pay to him. I try to bluff him, try to look uncertain and fidget when I've got a strong hand, sit still with a weak one, mix up the signals, but that guy can somehow read me. Must be something they learn in seminary."

***

I tried to push thoughts about the dead and wounded out of my mind. Repair what we can and go on to the next patient. What else is possible? When I was a resident in cardiac surgery, we often operated on high-risk infants. My professor only visited the families briefly the night before the surgery. If one of the kids died during the operation, the professor would have *us* talk to the family. He'd lock himself in his office until the next morning. At the time, I thought he was a coward, but now I can understand why he did it. Exhaustion from failure is different from exhaustion from endless work. Fatigue is helped by sleep. But failure requires searching for reasons and alternatives before proceeding with the next day's surgery.

***

After the sheets of rain and heavy winds cleared, the fighting resumed. Out to sea, toward Monkey Mountain, a helicopter's distant landing light appeared, turbine blades whomping at full throttle, flying over the ocean toward the hospital. We finally heard the noise and ran across the sand to the admissions ward. Father Perez was already there, sitting beside an unconscious Vietnamese boy with a deep head wound, holding the mother's hand. Colonel Thompson, the hospital chief, was standing by the communications radio in the admissions ward.

He looked at me. "An airborne medevac helicopter radioed they had picked up a soldier near Monkey Mountain with an unexploded rocket grenade in his chest. They're bringing him here. Arrival time is estimated in five minutes.

"We can't bring him into the operating rooms," the colonel added. "If the grenade blows, it'd destroy the whole surgical unit. Put the soldier in the morgue. You can operate on him there. We'll surround you with sandbags so that only your arms and head will be exposed."

"Oh fine, Colonel. I'll be sure to wear my uniform with my name on it so they can identify the torso."

"Well, hell, Major, what else can we do? And don't bring him into the goddamn X-ray department. Take the X-ray with the portable machine out on the helicopter pad. I've called an ordnance expert who's on his way here. Good luck." The colonel returned to his air-conditioned trailer.

The morgue's humid, still air held a nauseating odor of decay even though all the bodies had been moved to the hallway. The autopsy table, closely rimmed with sandbags, had been placed under a dim ceiling lamp. A nurse rapidly

sorted surgical instruments on a small table and then left
the room. The helicopter approached the hospital, slowed,
turned its nose into the wind, and lowered gradually while
blowing sheets of sand for a gentle landing. The wounded
soldier was buried under flak vests except for his wide-eyed
face. After the vests were removed, he was carefully placed
on a stretcher, floodlights then revealing a deep, bloody
chest wound. The helicopter quickly took off, leaving just
an orderly, Father Perez, and me with the patient outside
the hospital. Father, without a flak vest, placed his hand on
the soldier's forehead and whispered a short prayer. Two
nurses wearing helmets and vests stared from the entrance
of the admissions department. The X-ray taken with the
portable machine didn't show the grenade or much of the
soldier's anatomy. The colonel was nowhere in sight. I decided to move the soldier into the hospital where there was
a more powerful X-ray.

"We can't operate unless we know just where the grenade is."

A jeep with "Ordnance" painted on its bumper parked
on the edge of the helipad. The driver, armor- and helmet-
clad, ambled like a heavyweight wrestler into the hospital,
carrying a large metal box. "Who's the cutter?" he said. I
shook his huge hand.

"Now, Doc, this thing in his chest is about this shape,"
he said, drawing a large egg on a piece of paper. He pointed
as he continued his sketch. "And this propeller is at the
rear. That's how the grenade is armed; the propeller turns
and arms the rocket as it flies through the air. This one

didn't explode—maybe it hit the marine before the propeller had time to turn enough. Maybe it has to turn just a little more before it can explode. Or maybe it's just a dud."

He looked up from the drawing and over to me. "Major, I want you to be very careful when you remove this. Don't turn the propeller, even slightly. Don't pull or push on the grenade, and don't even think about dropping it. Just gently remove it and hand it to me." He smiled. "I'll be right behind you, and I'll put the grenade in the box and take it away. Got it?" Father Perez looked at me and patted the bottle of tequila in his pocket beside his holy water.

I looked around the morgue. The sandbags surrounding the autopsy table were placed so the surgeons could look over the top and put their arms through small openings to operate on the soldier.

"How could that work—how can we operate so far from the patient? If it blows up, we'll be dead like the soldier, headless and armless, but just as dead. Sandbags or no sandbags." I realized it would be impossible to operate with precision and extreme gentleness while standing behind sandbags. I also needed the patient completely paralyzed by the anesthetist and decided to make a large incision so we could remove the grenade without touching the propeller. We moved the sandbags away from the stretcher so they would be behind us instead of between the surgeons and the patient. The hospital would still be protected. Someone brought flak vests and helmets for the surgical team. As my vest was zipped closed, I thought about what Graham had been saying about chance and God watching over us. What would my wife and my children do if I didn't come home? I could no longer remember their voices—it had been so long.

For a moment, I could visualize Mimi and our children sitting beside my coffin in the Methodist sanctuary. Reverend Coleman standing starched and clean in the pulpit, his eyes searching the sanctuary ceiling in search of inspiration or any other help, his arms and scarlet scarf reaching out in intercession above my flag-draped box. His favorite hymns echoed from the sanctuary's stained glass. God help us all.

Graham walked into the morgue.

"I'm helping you—we're in this together," he said, assisting me with my vest and helmet.

"Jesus, Graham, thank you!"

I silently prayed—what I could remember of the Apostles' Creed:

I believe in God, the Father Almighty, creator of heaven and earth.

I believe in Jesus Christ, his only Son.

On the third day he rose again and ascended into heaven—

The surgical team was ready. A medic brought the second X-ray showing good details of the soldier's bones and marked swelling of soft tissues. But there was no grenade—just a few pieces of metal in the soldier's chest wall. The grenade must have bounced off the soldier's flak vest and not exploded despite hitting him hard. Maybe it had been defective. I showed the X-ray to the ordnance expert, who was standing outside the ring of sandbags, his face covered with a Plexiglas mask. He looked disappointed.

Father Perez was standing on the other side of the table inside the ring of sandbags, hands together, no flak vest or helmet, his uniform soaked with sweat. Our eyes met.

"Just some bleeding in the chest wall muscles," I said. Father nodded and again patted a bottle in his rear pocket.

I thought of Hemingway's story about a terrified soldier huddled in a trench, continuously praying to Jesus as bombs exploded, saying he loves him and believes in God and that he would always and forevermore be a disciple if God should spare his life.

He survives and the next night goes upstairs with a girl at the Villa Rossa and does not tell her or anyone else about Jesus.

Graham, smiling, looked relieved. "It's just fucking luck—but sometimes things work out," he said.

We looked for Father, who, a few moments ago, had given a thumbs-up and pointed to the tequila in one of his pockets. But he had returned to the Vietnamese mother with the brain-injured child. There were just a few nurses and medics in the admissions ward. Most had not yet returned from the rocket shelters. But Father was there; perspiration still ran off his glasses and dripped from his unruly hair. It soaked his shirt, steamed his glasses, and dripped onto his vestments while he leaned over the injured child.

On the wall above Perez was a sign from the CO's office

posted two days ago: "All personnel must wear proper military uniforms and salute appropriately. Failure to do so will result in fines and possible reassignments."

***

Later that night, a helicopter flew rapidly and low; its landing light illuminated the ground before settling on our helipad and shutting down its engine. Medics with stretchers ran toward the Huey. There was only one patient on board. His face was unrecognizable after being struck by a booby trap causing a severe facial wound with fractures of his mandible and facial bones. A medic from the helicopter helped unload the wounded soldier.

"He can only breathe lying on his stomach," he said.

The soldier was gasping for air even while lying on his stomach, inhaling with shrill whistling noises and exhaling a bloody froth. There was no way to insert a breathing tube through his mouth or nose because of the severe facial damage. He desperately needed an airway inserted into his trachea but was unable to breathe except when lying on his stomach. I lay on the helipad with several medics holding the soldier's head and neck overhead. Reaching up, I cut into the patient's neck while streams of blood dripped down onto my face and glasses. Finally, an opening into the trachea was made, and a tube was inserted into the windpipe. A violent coughing of blood sprayed down over my face and scrubs. This was the first time I had operated on a patient who was on top of me! With his breathing secured, the patient was taken to surgery, and his jaw and face were repaired. After months of combat surgery, I was comfortable thinking on my feet. Operating upside down was just what had been necessary. I cleaned off the blood and went back to our little room for a brief rest.

Lying on my cot, I thought about the German hospital ship again, the *Helgoland*. It was large, with 150 beds and ten doctors, and it was painted bright white with large red crosses. Anchored in the Han River near the center of Da Nang, it had never been hit by rocket or VC ground attacks that often occurred in that part of the city. There were no guards near the ship and no visible security posts. There must be an agreement between the Germans and the VC to care for their wounded. How else could the ship be untouched in the midst of rocket attacks and sabotage? It seemed so safe. How wonderful it would be if all hospitals were off limits for attacking, and civilians and wounded from both sides could be treated and sheltered there. No one had ever mentioned this possibility. I had visited the ship and met the German surgeons. They were pleasant but quite self-contained during a lunch of meat and potatoes, foods that I had almost forgotten about. I never returned to the *Helgoland*.

Our hospital's mission involved treating wounded soldiers. The numbers of these patients depended on the severity of combat within one hundred miles of Da Nang. When there was a lull in fighting, we also operated on civilian patients with problems unrelated to the war such as hernias, lungs damaged by infections, bowel cancers, accidental injuries, and cardiac mitral valves damaged from rheumatic fever.

From what I saw on my visit to the *Helgoland*, there were fewer and less-severe trauma admissions, but a significant number of elective surgical procedures. Several months before my visit to the ship, Dr. Phouc and I had started operating at our American army hospital on patients with hearts damaged by rheumatic fever. We had repaired three or four mitral valves successfully without a cardiopulmonary bypass machine when I learned that the thoracic surgeon on the German ship had also started repairing heart valves. Nothing like competition to improve the breed, I guess.

***

Earlier in the week, casualties had poured in from nearby heavy fighting, but now, as if everyone needed to rest and regroup, the explosions and gunfire had tapered off. I sat in a broken lawn chair and stared at a battleship five miles out to sea. With a flash of fire and a cloud of smoke, it fired a heavy shell that whistled over our hospital, exploding somewhere beyond the Da Nang airport miles away. I wondered how many people would die from that shell and assumed it would be better to die suddenly in the jungle rather than be seriously wounded and slowly bleed to death or die from an infection somewhere beyond help. We had been operating for three days without sleep. Now without much else to do except look at the warship and the more distant ocean's curve along the horizon, I thought about my boyhood experiences watching surgery, the years of surgical training, and the months of combat surgery that had changed my life and changed the way I thought about things.

Now I appreciated the guidance of my parents to do a job well and to persist until it was finished, at least as well as I could do it. That guidance had been uncomfortable, especially coming from my father. It had been premature, even out of place. But those hard-won habits had been valuable during my years of training and in Vietnam. I again thought about Dad never giving up, not even when playing golf, when we had to search in the weeds for his damn ball until he found it, not just any ball, but *his* ball. As a youngster, I had watched him operate many times, but had never seen him give up hope of saving someone with a complicated surgical problem. His attitude reminded me again how we had to find his ball even when we had seen it arch high in the air and sail far out of bounds. Little did I know then, it was attitude training for me, whether he realized it or not.

And I hoped to teach each of our children the value of persistence and the importance of doing a good job with whatever they tried to accomplish later in their life. Hopefully, their choices of career would be wise and we could offer them help if they asked us, or perhaps even offer occasional, unsolicited advice. But, for that, I would have to be careful to remain calm and reasonable, as difficult as that might be. Mimi would be better at that than I.

I had become an experienced and hopefully wiser combat surgeon. Most of the fighting occurred during the night or in the early-morning hours when it was easier for the VC to launch undetected attacks. I gradually changed from sleeping at night to remaining alert in the darkness and sleeping whenever possible during daylight hours.

During years of training, I had learned the fine details of anatomy and how to identify vital structures by feel instead of only by vision. We learned the advantages of different incisions and sutures for each surgical procedure. Above all, the importance of gentle, meticulous handling of body tissues was emphasized. The length of time to complete a surgical procedure had been of secondary importance.

Back then, I had performed surgery for several months in a rural Haitian hospital. An experienced surgeon was available for advice, but he was usually busy and had many other responsibilities. Making choices alone during surgery became more comfortable for me; precise knowledge of anatomy was essential. Later, that experience was a great help in performing combat surgery in Vietnam, where severe injuries required careful but rapid decisions and unusual approaches to damaged organs.

I had rarely encountered massive bleeding before the war. I learned about that as a combat surgeon. Successful combat surgery required rapid assessment of the wounded; the exact location of bleeding in the abdomen or chest was unknown before surgery. There wasn't time for a precise diagnosis. X-rays were slow to develop and often not helpful.

Stopping uncontrolled bleeding was the most important thing for patient survival. Control the bleeding any way that worked, but it had to be done quickly or the patient would be lost. Seconds of delay could be fatal.

Whatever part of the body was hiding severe bleeding was opened widely. Often, suction and blotting with sponges couldn't remove the blood quickly enough. Instead, it was rapidly scooped out by hands, cascading over the patient and the operating team, and splashing onto the operating-room floors. Continued bright red bleeding was then identified and sponges pushed firmly against it until the patient's blood pressure could be brought back to safe levels by more transfusions. The surgeon had to think about the anatomy under those sponges, about what might be damaged and need repair or removal. Rapid, logical thinking was critical. Massive bleeding was almost a daily experience; surgeons were easily identified as the blood-soaked doctors.

GETTING SHORT

Now I was getting "short." Usually that meant only a few weeks left in Vietnam. We all had calendars with 365 days to mark off; just a few unmarked days remained on mine. Just a few weeks until I would see my family. I missed Mimi, the kids, and our parents, but knew that thinking about leaving the war zone was a dangerous distraction. But I could no longer see them in my mind. Looking at photos helped, but when I slid them back into their envelopes, the images seemed to melt away. Without those photographs, I could no longer imagine what anyone at home looked like and could no longer see their faces in my mind. That worried me. What if Mimi and I had drifted apart because of all the stress we shared and the uncertainties of my returning? What about our undecided future? What if our children no longer knew or recognized me? Was bad news, perhaps about our parents' health, omitted from letters from home? I hadn't received a letter from Dad for more than a month.

There were many stories about "short" GIs getting wounded or killed—as if short brought a certain kind of danger, perhaps a loss of concentration. In previous months, several GIs told me about soldiers they had known who were killed in firefights just hours before they were supposed to return to their base camp for a helicopter ride to Da Nang and a flight back home. Their pockets held crumpled orders for flights home when their bodies were found after that one last patrol.

Working only in our hospital until it was time to leave Vietnam was not a guarantee of safety. A rocket meant for the nearby marine base might fall short and hit the hospital. Some had come very close. Or there might be an attack directly on the hospital from the sea, where we had very weak defenses—just two guard towers and several strings of razor wire. I decided to continue working at the Vietnamese hospitals and our army hospital, as always, until leaving for home. Changing routines, being extra careful, might expose unexpected dangers.

***

Monsoon season. The ocean's flat gray blended perfectly with the dull sky. Large waves crashed onto the beach, and water flooded the hospital floors. I couldn't hear gunfire or even helicopters, but they still landed with new casualties. Bomber pilots waited for breaks in the weather. I talked to them. They said each day they received orders from Washington politicians about targets to hit and the types of munitions they must carry. During daylight, trucks loaded with military supplies for the VC parked in plain sight in North Vietnamese villages declared off-limits to bombing. One major, a pilot I had talked with frequently, did not return from a mission. Marine casualties arrived after taking the same hill near Da Nang for the third time this year. Fifty boots of the dead again lined the admissions wall. Slippery blood covered the floors.

The *Stars and Stripes* newspaper wrote about favorable body counts. Hanoi Hannah broadcast daily on my short-wave radio:

"Yank, why you fight this war? You get wounded or killed for what? No one trusts Saigon government. Not worth life. Go home. Girlfriends and wives lonesome; many men keep them company."

She listed names and hometowns of GIs recently killed and played songs like Pete Seeger's "Where Have All the Flowers Gone?"

I think Hanoi Hannah's broadcasts are closer to the truth.

"GI, is very good idea to leave a sinking ship. You know you cannot win this war."

I imagined how devastating it would be as a parent to have a son killed taking the same hill for the third time because of some theory about how favorable body counts were discouraging the enemy. VC kills would be announced—whatever that meant. Did the count include anyone in black pajamas or anyone running instead of walking? Who was actually killed? A farmer, a VC, or some frightened villager? One thing the parent would know if his soldier son was killed in action: his son was part of the sacrifice for that body count, killed for a military theory that, so far, hadn't worked out.

Cold rain roared horizontally across the hospital. I counted my remaining days on a wall calendar and again checked the .32 pistol, now hidden in my right boot. I slept in a body bag, thankful for its warmth.

A few more days passed; the rain stopped, and the gray sky cleared. *The Graduate* movie projected on one of the hospital's outside white Quonset walls. We sat in the nearby sand. Many of us had been working for almost twelve months and were talking about going home and getting the hell out of Da Nang. There were lots of ribald comments about the film; hand motions from the audience were projected onto the screen, gripping parts of Mrs. Robinson as she spoke in her low, beckoning voice and sauntered across the screen. Someone shouted, "Wait; stop the movie; that's my wife!" Some soldiers, bored with the movie, threw rocks at rats gathered between the mess hall and hospital in near darkness.

A corpsman suddenly came running across the sand toward us from the receiving section of the hospital, shouting, "Incoming medevacs! Incoming casualties!" All the docs and nurses got up off the sand and ran toward the receiving ward. Helicopters flew fast and low over the South China Sea to our hospital. Coming closer, their red crosses faintly visible, they braked aggressively with abrupt nose-up movements and landed quickly. The pilots, as if still searching for enemy soldiers, did not move from their seats and kept the turbines and rotor blades powered and ready for takeoff. Medics ran to the nearest Huey, opening the side doors to the wounded. The screams of men and machines made communication impossible. One soldier got off by himself, clutching what was left of his left arm. Two others had no heartbeats and were placed in a corner of the helipad. Another soldier was breathing and rapidly taken into the hospital for careful examination. His bloody, mud-soaked uniform and boots were removed. His blood-filled abdomen bulged. The soldier answered weakly to the name on his dog tag: Jesse. He reached down to his abdomen to indicate where it hurt the most. Then, he suddenly had a major seizure. I examined his head carefully—there was no wound. Large-bore needles were being inserted into his arms. Someone shouted as donor blood arrived from across the hall. "He's type AB!" Blood was started in each arm and infused under pressure. It was not the first time we had seen seizures in soldiers with very low blood pressures. In less than a minute, he was lifted onto an operating table; iodine was rapidly painted on the soldier's abdomen and a tube placed in his trachea. I made a cut vertically along the entire length of the abdomen as the anesthetic was begun. Clotted and liquid blood was scooped out of the abdomen, running across the sterile sheets, overfilling catch basins, splashing over our legs and feet. Sponges were held tightly against the bright bleeding in the upper abdomen as the transfusions continued. Sweat trickled down my glasses and dripped into the wound. The blood pressure was forty. After the first two bags of blood were given, others were immediately started—and pumped in, until the pressure climbed to eighty. Sponges were carefully peeled away from the upper abdomen. Suddenly, bright bleeding began in the left upper quadrant. The shattered spleen was scooped out of the abdomen, its entire blood supply clamped off with a large hemostat and a single suture. But significant bleeding continued from the stomach's many tears and from the damaged pancreas. The stomach was wrapped in sponges while the pancreas was mobilized and half of it removed. Then, the middle portion of the stomach was removed, and the remaining parts were sutured back together.

"I still can't get the pressure up above eighty," the Sultan said.

"Hell, I thought we were out of trouble."

I searched for more problems. More bright blood was collecting in the upper abdomen again and now appeared to be coming from a small wound of the diaphragm. The wound was enlarged, and a quart of blood was rapidly suctioned out of the left chest.

"Well, the lung's ok, but there's a tear in the pericardium." The diaphragm was incised farther for better visibility of the heart from within the abdomen. A medic held up the sternum with large retractors so the tissue sac around the heart, the pericardium, was visible through the abdominal incision and the opened left diaphragm. Blood was spurting from a tear in the pericardium. When this was opened, a stream of blood could be seen streaming from the heart with each beat.

Princess, the nurse with perfume and dangly earrings, pushed against me to see. The way she crowded closely might have been a pleasant experience under other circumstances, but the closeness of the perfume vapors and the banging of her earrings meant she thought we were in serious trouble. She was trying to see exactly where the bleeding was coming from in order to quickly hand me the most useful instruments. It was a floral barometer of our troubles.

"I'll be damned. There are two holes in the left ventricle, one on each side of the anterior coronary artery!"

There was one chance to get out of trouble: a deep suture on each side of the artery. If either suture tore the heart muscle, massive bleeding would occur that couldn't be stopped without a heart-lung machine—unavailable in Vietnam. Small Dacron patches were used to anchor the sutures on each side of the two cardiac wounds. Very gradually the ties were cinched down; the bloody stream slowed and finally stopped completely. The blood pressure came up to normal. I looked around the surgical Quonset Hut, for the first time aware that all the five other tables were occupied with wounded having emergency procedures.

The patient was stable and appeared reasonably comfortable in the morning. Because of the soldier's multiple severe injuries, including the cardiac wounds, the hospital commanding officer thought I should fly with this patient to Letterman Hospital in San Francisco, where open-heart surgery was available if needed. I would be leaving one day short of my year assignment to Vietnam. It was very unusual to survive a cardiac wound in combat. I could think of only one other similar wound since I had arrived in Vietnam.

***

We didn't often talk with our patients after surgery. As soon as they were stable, they were discharged and evacuated to Japan, Okinawa, or back to the States. We could usually save the lives of the injured soldiers, but because I found it upsetting to contemplate their future, I often avoided talking with them and was relieved when they left the hospital. So many tragic stories. We had done what we could, but I thought many of their futures were uncertain.

During my training as a surgical resident, I had worked at a veterans' hospital and taken care of some patients with long-standing injuries from previous wars. Besides playing cards or watching television in the ward's sunrooms, their days consisted of visits to physical therapy, nurses giving scheduled medicines, or orderlies helping them into and out of chairs or wheelchairs so they could take an elevator down to the smoke-layered lobby for a cigarette or two.

A few clergy greeted the patients in their rooms, shared short prayers, and then proceeded down the hall, crossing names off their lists. Some soldiers had been in the hospital for years since their wounding. They ironically called it their redbrick mother. There were seldom visits from family or friends.

I hoped this would not happen to the young, bright soldiers I had operated on, but the end result of serving their country and suffering complicated injuries in an unpopular war was sometimes going to be long-term hospitalization in a veterans' hospital. For many, there was no other option. Politicians never visited or talked about these patients; they just talked about taking care of "our" veterans without knowing what happened to these soldiers as the months and years passed by.

Two days before I was to fly home, I walked through several postoperative wards. I decided to listen to some of the stories that I had avoided earlier in the year while trying to avoid the stress of their horrors. But now, I thought some of the stories might be useful if I someday wanted to write about a surgeon's experience in Vietnam. I hadn't yet realized how permanent the memories of the close calls and near-death experiences would remain in my mind and the minds of other soldiers who had survived that year. Fifty years later when I met Vietnam veterans, I would still listen to vivid stories that seemed to have happened just days ago.

In the ward reserved for patients with minor wounds, soldiers dressed in blue pajamas were kneeling on the floor around an empty stretcher, shouting as they slapped cards down and rolled dice on the canvas. I didn't think they wanted to talk about combat injuries, at least not then, so I continued down the concrete hallway to a ward reserved for severely injured patients. One injured soldier was lying on a cot near the entrance. One of his bandages was saturated with wound drainage. I replaced it with a dry dressing while we talked. Grimacing while tears streaked down his sutured face, he asked me, "Well, Doc, how will this end up?"

His left arm was taped to a padded board to secure an IV. He used his right arm to point to the large gauze dressing covering his abdomen and his colostomy. Another bulky bandage over his crotch covered an extensive loss of tissue, including most of his penis. I had heard about his severe injuries from several surgeons who had operated on him two nights ago. Urine dribbled through a clear plastic catheter to a bag that hung on the bed frame.

I had noticed most soldiers who arrived still conscious at our hospital with wounds of the lower abdomen or upper legs checked their penises for damage.

"I don't care how I'll look," he said, "I can even learn to use a new arm and shit into a bag. But what kind of a job can I get? Who would want me now?"

Then the last question: "Will I ever be able to fuck my woman again?"

I listened to his questions and stared at the concrete floor while he talked. I had not thought about losing a penis in this damn war. I tried but couldn't imagine how I would react if I had suffered a similar injury. That injury would be even more depressing for a young infantry soldier. I had heard about plastic surgical procedures to repair these injuries, but the type of injury, and whether there was significant tissue loss, must determine the success of even skilled reconstructions. Fighting tears, I looked up at him and answered as best I could.

"It will take time and more surgery. But if she doesn't stand by you, and can't help you recover or adjust to changes, there are many women who would.

"I'll ask Father Perez to talk with you later today."

I wondered what Perez might say about losing a penis, sexual intercourse, and miracles.

***

In Dad's war, soldiers with these massive injuries would have bled to death on the battlefields. An important purpose of those hospitals was to return as many wounded soldiers as possible to fighting and defeating the Germans. Especially during the most intense fighting, some severely wounded soldiers who reached hospitals were given narcotics to ease their suffering but were not taken to surgery because there were not enough surgeons, hospitals, or blood. Time was vital. More soldiers with relatively minor wounds could return to the fighting after surgery than could those few returning after repair of their massive injuries. It was a cold, hard fact. The outcomes of combat at times depended then on the available number of soldiers available to fight. Extensive use of rehabilitation wasn't necessary then.

But in Vietnam, we tried to save almost everybody who arrived at our hospital alive, no matter how severe their injuries. I really didn't know what would happen to them in the future. I tried to be optimistic, but could not lie to them. Most of the wounded were young, eighteen to twenty years old. They had no job or profession before they joined the army, and no way to move on with their lives after the war without extensive training that would be difficult or impossible because of their injuries and further hospitalizations.

I had no experience with multiple reconstructive surgical procedures, but wasn't certain that saving someone with such debilitating injuries was the best thing to do after taking care of soldiers from previous wars during my residency. Multiple operative procedures, multiple medications in veterans' hospitals still hadn't helped enough to enable some of these soldiers to lead normal lives. Their old injuries had made them dependent on the care system despite multiple attempts to improve their function. And a soldier might not have wanted his life to be saved if he had been able to choose. But who can foresee the future? No one can always make the most desirable choice for a wounded soldier's life. Often decisions in the operating rooms were made in a few seconds, and sometimes the results were very depressing.

Despite Father Perez's belief in the value of a person's soul, sometimes all choices for life were bad. Even so, we rarely chose to treat a soldier with narcotics only and not offer a chance to save his life. I sought relief by returning to the operating rooms, avoiding most other people, and sharing the horrors only with other surgeons. Perhaps this lack of connection, this avoidance, helped me control the stress of operating on these seriously injured patients even though, in the operating rooms, I knew they had little chance of resuming their previous lives.

I learned that the patient whose heart I had repaired came from a small Iowa farm not far from my boyhood home. His name was Jesse Granger, a sergeant in the infantry. I wanted to follow his course over the next months and make certain he did well. I was the only physician who had seen his damaged heart, the one who had repaired it with a technique I had never heard of. I decided to talk with him before we left the hospital for San Francisco. I thought careful follow-up would be necessary to detect a functional narrowing of the anterior coronary artery or to detect a possible bulge, an aneurysm, of the heart because of the sutures I had placed in the cardiac muscle. I saw him sitting up in his bed near the entrance of one of the surgical critical-care wards.

"Hey, Jesse, how are you feeling today? I'm the doctor who operated on you the other night."

"Thanks, Doc. The nurses said you saved my life. Will I ever be normal, though? They said there were lots of holes in the bowel and stomach, and you had to remove my spleen. And how about my heart? Will I be able to work hard on our farm? Can I give my dad a hand? He's been needing help the past few years."

Two medevac helicopters then flew low over the hospital; the vibrating roar of jet engines shook the soldier's bed and caused us both to duck.

"Jesse, the bowel and stomach wounds are repaired. The loss of your spleen shouldn't cause problems, and your heart is healing well. The EKG, your blood pressure, and heart rhythm are all normal." I could feel a rising anxiety while I talked. I couldn't tell him, without doubt, that his heart would be fine. If that coronary artery had been narrowed with the closure of heart muscle, Jesse could have a heart attack. He was just nineteen and had suffered a near-death experience while that night I had improvised a repair that I had never seen or heard of. Using large curved needles, two sutures had been placed through the entire thickness of the heart muscle, under the perforations and the coronary artery into the left ventricular chamber, and then back to the heart surface on the other side of the wounds and the artery. The sutures were then tied firmly enough to close the perforations, but not tight enough to stop blood flow through the coronary artery. I would have to tell the doctors at Letterman about Jesse's injury, the surgical details, and my concerns about his future.

Another medevac landed with a roar and clouds of sand.

"We're both returning to San Francisco the day after tomorrow. I'll go with you to Letterman Hospital and get you checked in. I imagine after a few days you will be transferred to the veterans' hospital in Iowa City. I think you will be fine," I said, "but you will need to be followed closely by cardiologists for a few years."

I began walking back to my hooch. A medic ran toward me. "Major Meffert," he said, "we need you in surgery immediately; one of our new surgeons can't get the bleeding stopped in a soldier's neck." We ran to the operating rooms. I stepped around large clots on the floor and looked over the surgeon's shoulder while he told me the details.

"This guy had a huge piece of shrapnel lodged in his neck and jammed under his jaw. I clamped off the carotid artery and jugular vein below, but when the metal was removed, dark blood shot out from the skull!" A black jagged, brick-sized shell fragment lay on the instrument table behind the scrub technician.

The surgeon was pushing a small pack of gauze deep into the wound against the bottom of the patient's skull.

"Can you remove the pack and use a finger or thumb to stop the bleeding so we can see exactly where the blood is coming from?" I asked.

He pulled the pack away, and dark blood shot out of the skull as if from a pressurized garden hose, stopping only when he pressed his thumb firmly into a hole in the soldier's skull. The dark blood had to be venous bleeding, and the only thumb-sized vein in that location was the jugular vein.

"Jesus, I can't move my thumb—the guy will bleed to death!"

"That's a hell of a way to go stateside—a pair of conjoined twins! It's the jugular," I said. "It's the jugular vein sheared off where it exits the skull."

"Well, there are two of them, a left and a right," he said.

"They join inside the skull before they enter the neck. One jugular can be ligated during neck surgery without problems," I added. "The only chance of control is to plug the vein opening tightly. A strip of vaginal packing should be narrow enough to push up into the skull."

A medic went to one of the supply cabinets and returned with a tube of the sterile gauze.

"Take the end of this with a forceps in your other hand and remove your thumb just a little at a time while you push as much of it as you can into the hole of the skull. If you can put at least two feet of it in there, I think you will be able to reclaim your thumb. Bring the end of the pack out of the upper corner of the skin incision."

The bleeding stopped after the pack was forced into the skull. Everyone relaxed.

I could imagine a blood clot starting to form just above the pack in the patient's jugular vein. It would probably become firm and rubbery in a day or two and in a few days, firm enough to permanently close that jugular vein.

"You might want to remove the pack a few inches each day, starting next week when I'll be gone."

The surgeon looked at me and grinned.

Making rapid decisions after a quick mental review of the involved anatomy had become a reflex frequently called upon during the year of combat surgery. It had been useful in Haiti where I first performed surgery alone while a resident, but it was essential in Vietnam. I hoped this newly arrived surgeon would learn quickly.

***

The following day, Dr. Phouc came to our hospital to visit preoperative patients who had returned to the tent beside our admissions ward after disappearing during the recent fighting. I introduced him to several surgeons newly arrived in the country who, I hoped, would continue to perform complicated civilian surgery at our American hospital with Dr. Phouc. He was now more serious, with rare smiles, but said his family was safe and that no one had been injured in the recent attacks.

I made rounds with him at the civilian Vietnamese hospital for the final time. The stench, the crowded beds, patients lying on floors, the lack of running water or indoor toilets—nothing had changed in almost twelve months. Dr. Phouc and I had, instead of using the civilian hospital, operated on Vietnamese patients with major surgical problems at our evacuation hospital, and the results had been good. I hardly recognized several women working with patients at the civilian hospital. They smiled, gave a thumbs-up, and walked briskly past us down the aisle of the surgical ward.

"Remember those two?" Phouc asked me.

"No," I answered.

"Those were the first patients whose hearts we operated on. You opened their mitral valves. Before surgery, they had severe shortness of breath and could barely walk. Now look at them!"

Dr. Phouc and I finished rounds and exchanged gifts of surgical books. He sent one with me to give to my father. I read the flyleaf:

To Dr. Clyde Meffert, thank you very much for giving me an easy, popular, and noble friend, a number one surgeon, Dr. William Meffert.

My gift to him was a book about surgical treatment of trauma.

To Dr. Phouc, my surgical partner. Thanks for your energy and your bravery. We will be friends forever.

There were tears, heartfelt goodbyes, and a final hug. Neither one of us thought we would ever see each other again.

It was dark when my driver and I started back to our hospital. The road wound through Da Nang near the airport.

"Do you want to stay in the barracks at the airport tonight, sir?" he asked. "In the morning, you would just have to walk across a runway, show your orders, and get on a jet to the States."

"Thanks, but I'll go back to the hospital tonight and

take an early-morning medevac to the airport with the soldier I operated on last week. I have some packing to do and need to see old friends one last time."

I returned to the room Graham and I had shared. I decided to leave all my fatigues in the room and the next day wear boots and my khaki uniform home. Just a few clothes packed in my duffel bag, several vases made from spent howitzer casings, my camera, and Dad's pistol, which I placed in a concealed part of my camera case. Then I headed to the small officers' club for a going-away party.

**

Shouting and hugging, nurses, doctors, and medics crowded inside the smoky, stone-walled officers' club.

"See you at the reunions! See you again in a few years!"

I suppose those walls would have protected us from small-arms fire, but certainly not from rockets or the showers of stone fragments from a direct hit.

I toasted "the Sultan," who still gave his anesthetics with a towel wrapped around his bald head.

"Looking like a king must have worked, Sult. Don't change; you're getting short. I'd wear the towel all the way to San Francisco!"

Then "the Princess," with the perfume and dangly earrings, gave me a special, close hug, the bouncing noises of her metal earrings, the pungent perfume, the kisses and tears. I would miss her especially.

"See you at the reunions! See you at the reunions!" We repeated it over and over, but each toast made it even less easy to leave. We had helped each other through the bad times, and we knew we probably would never see each other again.

I was up and packed by three o'clock in the morning. I checked on Jesse, the patient I was accompanying to San Francisco. He was stable and anxious to start home. We waited in the admissions building. Soon rotor blades clapped into the quiet night; then came a light and a roar of jet engines as the Huey approached and touched down on the hospital pad. We pushed Jesse's gurney out to the copter and strapped him to the floor. It wasn't a medevac; there was no red cross on its side. I shoved my duffel and camera case under the bench seat and sat down opposite the open sliding door on the left side of the helicopter. No one else was in that side of the helicopter. I felt for a safety belt in the darkness but couldn't find one. We took off, nosed down to gain speed, and climbed into the darkness. In a few minutes, the airport was visible, and we could see a burning, crushed building near the main runway. It was the transient building that I had decided not to stay in earlier in the night!

Then the helicopter's nose pitched up, the jet engines throttled back, and we began to lose speed and altitude for a landing. Suddenly there was a brilliant flash just in front and below us. The helicopter banked sharply onto its left side in a steep turn. We were about five hundred feet above the airport. The pilot turned the machine sharply and headed toward the ocean. I was looking directly down at the ground. There was not enough speed for centrifugal force to keep me in my seat; I began sliding toward the open door despite grabbing the seat edge. My boots were at the edge of the open door and still slipping out. In the dim light, I saw a vertical mounting bar for a machine gun near the front of the door opening. I thought of the irony of dying by falling out of the black sky on my final day in Vietnam. My final day. No one would know what happened; I would have just vanished. That thought was more fearsome than the knowledge I was going to die. A search would find nothing except my duffel bag crammed under the seat. I would never see my family again. Being lost forever flashed through my mind. It was overpowering, something I would have thought as I fell into the dark ocean. I had seen videos of people plunging uncontrollably from cliffs or from tall buildings, desperately trying to escape fires, their arms and legs flailing wildly. One of my boots now was out of the helicopter. Desperate, I grabbed the machine-gun mount in a double-arm lock and hung like a flag still attached to its pole in a gale-force wind. Even if my arms were torn, I would not let go. Now we were flying rapidly in blackness. Then the helicopter turned back to the airport, flying straight, fast, and level. I could see runway lights and the burning transient building again. The slipstream may have pushed me back inside the cabin. Or did someone grab me and pull me back into the cabin? I would never know. We landed uneventfully near the burning building.

I looked at the pilot through the window of the cockpit. I wanted to thank him. Sharp turns in near total darkness required special skills in maintaining control by relying on instruments instead of the horizon or visible landmarks. But the pilot kept the jet engines running, looked straight ahead, and soon took off. I have thought about the odds of surviving that night many times since then. Most medevac helicopters I had seen didn't have machine-gun mounts. The Huey we rode in was equipped for transporting soldiers into and away from battles. Why hadn't a medevac without machine-gun mounts been assigned that night to take us to the airport? How many helicopter pilots could have maintained control during the steep turns we made in total darkness over the ocean? Call it fate; call it luck. And why had I chosen to return to the hospital to say goodbyes instead of just checking into the transient building? I had seen these yes / no choices many times in Vietnam. Simple, innocent decisions that brought either life or death. For me, that was the most frightening danger. There was no defense and no way to avoid them in the unsecured combat zone.

I suppose Dad must have had similar close calls when the Germans captured his hospital in Belgium. He never talked about that.

In Vietnam, dangers happened suddenly and were followed by relative safety. The violence of the transient building destruction; the desperate clutching of the machine-gun mount as the helicopter turned steeply to avoid rocket explosions. Suddenly now, it was quiet and still dark. People acted as if everything were normal, as if the attacks were fantasy; they carried on as usual. I remember taking my duffel bag and camera case into the departure building at the airport and unfolding my orders to accompany Jesse home. I remember moving my arms and legs, flexing my body before boarding the jet. Except for scrapes and soreness of my arms, I seemed to have escaped serious injury, but thoughts of sliding out of that helicopter, to then vanish into the ocean without a trace and never see Mimi, our children, or our parents again, still persist. Even fifty years later, these memories are fresh and occur without warning, usually in the darkness just before dawn.

I must have checked on Jesse; we must have talked about the close calls, maybe even joked about them, but my mind is blank about our conversations while we waited to board the giant red-crossed airplane. I remember sitting on a long canvas bench fastened to the body of the airplane opposite Jesse, who lay on a stretcher with other wounded soldiers in the center of the aircraft. Two vertical stacks of wounded soldiers on stretchers were arranged three or four high along the entire aircraft. I sat at arm's length from the wounded, close to my patient. The foul, moist heat from the packed, wounded patients must have been overpowering. I don't remember that either, but it was something I had experienced in the hospitals and during previous flights accompanying patients to Japan. I do remember the rear clam doors' slowly closing, the engines' revving, and my breathing deeply as foggy, cool air rushed from aircraft vents. Then the clumsy taxiing for takeoff and our slow acceleration down the runway. I thought that we were still vulnerable, especially in the slow-moving C-141 aircraft. The heavy, drab jet hammered along the rough runway before lifting slowly into the humid air, leaving behind the stench of burning charcoal, rotten fish, and kerosene. I must have held my breath during liftoff, but before my eyes as we climbed into the clean air, the green, dangerous jungle transformed into an exotic travel-poster landscape. A few minutes after leveling off, the pilot announced we were leaving Vietnam and were now over the international waters of the South China Sea. The shouts and cheers were deafening. My patient, Jesse, looked comfortable but wasn't yet able to drink enough for his adequate hydration. I checked his IV and calculated that it was running at about 80 cc per hour. His blood pressure was 130 / 80, his temperature was normal, and the breath sounds were clear and unlabored when I listened to his lungs with my stethoscope. I relaxed against the back of my seat.

Jesse looked at me across the narrow aisle.

"Doc, you asked me what happened that night you saw me after I was wounded."

"Only if you want to talk about it," I answered, still in a state of shock and not wanting right then to hear more about this damn war or even listen to soldiers who had survived the fighting. A few weeks ago, I would have answered, *Maybe later*, and returned to the operating rooms to avoid the stress of combat stories. But we were flying over the ocean and away from Vietnam. I leaned closer to hear exactly what Jesse said. He began by talking about patrolling near the Ho Chi Minh Trail, but there was so much noise from the jet engines and from the outside air rushing along the sides of the aircraft that I missed most of his words, and we thought maybe we could talk about his platoon after we landed.

I sat back on the bench seat and wrote a few notes about this night and the day before. I had been lucky. Play it again, make those choices of meeting Dr. Phouc at the civilian hospital, exchanging gifts, the night travel back through Da Nang by jeep to our evacuation hospital rather than staying in the transient building, the helicopter ride back to the airport in darkness with Jesse, the near miss of a rocket, the pilot's ability to control the helicopter while escaping by flying over the South China Sea in complete darkness, the use of a combat helicopter with a machine-gun mounting bar for medical transport rather than a medevac; it had all been so fortuitous. I knew those choices, each vital, probably would not be chosen in sequence again if the past twenty-four hours had been somehow replayed. Looking at the stacks of wounded in the aircraft, I thought they, too, had been lucky even though some would not be able to function as they had before Vietnam. And the large numbers of dead and wounded enemy soldiers—I grieved for them also. Political decisions had made us enemies. I had operated on many of them, and they had been grateful to survive their injuries. We should have been in the same army. The soldiers from both sides just wanted peace, security for their families, and honest governments. Thousands of dead and wounded had been sacrificed, but soldiers from both sides had wanted the same things. Politicians should have to fight in wars they cause by persisting with stubborn demands. But how is an ordinary person to know what is a just cause, what is worth fighting for? Often the truth is available only after the fighting ceases. And, after most wars, soldiers from both sides eventually become friends and work together. I was very discouraged.

After an hour or so, one of the flight nurses mentioned to me that the plane was going to land in Okinawa to refuel and to load additional IV fluids, medicines, and meals for the longer flight to San Francisco. We must have taken off from Da Nang with less than a full load of fuel and fewer medical supplies to shorten our takeoff distance and allow a more rapid climb to decrease exposure to enemy rockets and small-arms fire.

The wounded were unloaded and taken to a nearby medical center in Okinawa while the airplane took on the supplies. I stayed near the airport, expecting a quick turnaround, but we were in Okinawa and out of the combat zone. Everything seemed to happen in slow motion and with less urgency. Everyone saluted and wore proper military attire. Perhaps knowing that a possible discipline for disobeying regulations might be a transfer to Vietnam, there was careful compliance with all the reminders and rules posted on the airport walls.

After a few hours, we left the island and resumed flying to California. Jesse had no problems even though, besides his diaphragm and heart, some injuries involved his stomach and intestines. One concern was that soldiers with gut

injuries might not yet have enough peristalsis to evacuate gas from their intestines and the gas would expand at
lower airplane cabin pressures. That expansion inside the
abdomen could be enough to interfere with their breathing and even tear open the abdominal incision. That was
one reason patients with these injuries were usually kept
in Vietnam a few days longer than other wounded soldiers.

We cruised smoothly along, high over the Pacific
Ocean. I was cold, something I hadn't experienced except
during the monsoon season one night when I crawled into
a body bag to block the heavy, horizontal rains. Now everyone was wrapped in blankets. Most of the patients
slept, including Jesse. I looked at the soldiers on stretchers stacked high in the airplane's center. Most were very
young, probably still in their late teens or early twenties.
Their futures must have been unplanned before entering
the army. I worried about them.

Few would have a job or a profession to come home
to. I suppose most of them would have families that loved
them, but there wasn't much else to help these wounded
soldiers recover and eventually lead successful lives. They
would be in veterans' hospitals and that would help their
physical recovery, but in my experience with these hospitals, living there with unresolved injuries became a way of
life for some patients—a substitute for returning to a normal life as a civilian, a sort of a halfway house that was
all some soldiers with serious unresolved injuries could
look forward to after their friends and sometimes even
their families drifted away. I worried that severe long-term

depression would occur in those chronically disabled patients from Vietnam who had survived severe battle injuries because of rapid helicopter evacuation and modern surgery.

I knew if my Methodist minister from home were here in this jet, he would be walking slowly along the narrow aisles and praying. *Lord, holy above all others, give us the strength to face this trial. We come to you, Jesus, when it seems like we can't go on. Give us strength . . . God cares for the sparrow. He is aware when the smallest of sparrows falls to the ground.*

But what would God actually do?

Raised a midwestern boy, I was trained to see things with a practical eye and then to react. In Iowa, there were always changing seasons to prepare for, urgent needs to be met. I was definitely not a mystic. I never had seen God reach out to a sparrow and doubted if anyone else had either.

Father Perez came from somewhere in the Southwest. He was a Catholic. But where he came from and even what he said weren't important to me. He had been one of us; he stayed with us during the worst of times. When others were in rocket shelters, he would be beside us, only sometimes helmeted and wearing a flak jacket. Except for his vestments, he was like the rest of us and brought comfort to the living, placed his hands on bloodied faces, asked for family names, and gave last rites to the dying. Despite what our Methodist preacher had professed when I was a teenager—that eternal life was just around the corner, a short distance from death—I didn't know if I believed in eternal life anymore. Sorting the mangled wounded from those dead and dying impressed upon me that life was precious, finite, and worth preserving almost at all costs. But, unlike Perez, I had a hard time believing in souls that needed to be saved no matter how grievous the injuries.

These soldiers were often just teenagers with only a high school education. They had seen buddies blown up beside them and body parts scattered in trees; they harbored horrible, unforgettable images. There was no psychological evaluation before returning to the States, and unlike after World War II, when soldiers waited in Europe often for weeks before boarding ships to slowly return home, the Vietnam veterans had often fought in Asian jungles just a day or two before returning to San Francisco.

Seeing hundreds of wounded soldiers and civilians had changed my mind about this war. Tens of thousands of Americans had lost their lives believing they were saving democracy (whatever that meant in the jungles and hamlets). Our government, our presidents, had told soldiers they were preventing a domino collapse of freedom in Vietnam and Southeast Asia. I read the *Stars and Stripes* articles about favorable outcomes in the fighting, as if body counts told the truth and could predict victory. But working at the evacuation hospital in Da Nang, I saw hills taken and given up and then taken again. Each time American lives were lost. Fallen Vietnamese men were included in the VC body counts whether or not they were enemy soldiers. If they wore black, if they ran, if they were outside at night, they were VC. During one year, our soldiers were ordered to take the same hill near our hospital three times. Three times, our hospital took heavy casualties, and twenty or thirty of our soldiers were killed in the fight for the hill. Each time, slippery blood covered the admissions ward's floor, and blood clots soaked piles of weapons, seeping into combat clothing and boots that had been hurriedly cast aside to make room for injured soldiers. We were told it was a victory each time the hill was "liberated." The VC had suffered more casualties, but after a year, the hill remained contested, and it seemed to me that our dead and wounded had gained nothing except unverified "favorable body counts" that pleased those who thought those counts would win the war. But I never saw a general or a politician visit our hospital admissions ward during heavy fighting, and if I had been a father of a dead soldier who was part of those favorable counts, I would have been confused and angry with the war's conduct and with our leaders. And I was no longer a midwestern boy who trusted those in command. I no longer respected politicians and generals conducting this war, and thought that I had been wrong to have once thought that government officials knew what was best for me or for our country. I was emotionally upset about the conduct and the original reasons given for entering this war and didn't talk to others about it.

Surgery became my salvation. Trying to salvage lives from this endless war, I decided that after this, I would organize my own surgical practice as independently as possible and not be told by CEOs, politicians, or generals what to do.

Like us, the Vietnamese just wanted their families to be safe; they wanted to work in their fields or at their jobs during the day and come home to their families and rest in the evening. I had listened to our translators who told me variants of this story countless times after talking with Vietnamese soldiers and civilians. As in other wars, soldiers from both sides could probably be friends if they survived the fighting. It was a political war sustained by political mistakes and stubborn politicians who had made promises and thought they needed to win the war to be reelected.

I thought about Dad's war, World War II. The Nazis tried to defeat Europe, Russia, and England; they murdered millions of people they thought inferior. Their armies and machines looked undefeatable. Hitler and his Nazis were feared and hated. There was no doubt that they had to be stopped, whatever the cost. When my father was a doctor with Patton's army, he carried that small pistol for self-defense and hated the German SS troops unless they were wounded. But he treated the wounded German soldiers as he treated his other patients and, a few years after the war, he drove a Volkswagen.

In Vietnam, we feared the VC but operated on them when they arrived, wounded, at our hospital. Both sides had sometimes tortured their enemies, and both sides had shown little mercy while in combat. But I had no doubt that, after the shootings and ambushes were finished, we would eventually become friends, just as we had become friends with the Germans and their allies. I didn't hate individual enemy soldiers. They had been inducted or forced into their army. We had been drafted. But all of us just wanted to end the fighting and return home. Still, each night before sleeping, I had carefully loaded my rifle and .45 pistol and laid them beside my cot next to a helmet and my flak vest.

**

The jet made a hard landing at Hickam Air Base in Honolulu, and I jolted awake. There were few windows in the C-141, so the hit of the wheels against the runway was a surprise. I thought perhaps we had struck something or been hit by ground fire. I fumbled with Dad's .32 pistol that pressed coldly against my chest under my shirt. The leather strap holding it to my neck had twisted. It was hot and humid on the ground. Either Guam or Hawaii, I didn't care. I thought about that gun. Each day in Vietnam I had packed it but never shot it. Pressing against my chest, it had been a comforting piece of lethal jewelry. Sometime after Tet, when downtown Da Nang was not safe, I had pulled it from under my shirt and aimed it at a group of solemn, possibly angry people who crowded close to my jeep while driving to the civilian hospital. They then looked frightened and moved away. Seriously outnumbered, I was frightened too.

Then we took off once again, flying high in smooth, cold air to California. Most patients, including Jesse, were sleeping. The roar and whine of jet engines was isolating. Conversation was difficult. I thought about home. Would I make it back to Iowa tonight or have to wait until tomorrow? I knew it would take time to get Jesse checked into Letterman Hospital and to explain his injuries to the surgeons stationed there.

I wondered who would meet me at the airport in Iowa. I had written letters to Mimi about coming home soon, perhaps next month, but there had been no recent phone connection available. Then Jesse had been injured, and the hospital commander asked me to fly home with him in case there was a problem with his heart or his other injuries. My family couldn't know I might be home early. I would call them from California. Thinking about meeting the family at the airport caused anxiety.

As a combat surgeon, I had held back emotions for months. I had buried them with additional surgery. Just moved on and hadn't talked with patients and, until a few days ago, had avoided stories about firefights, the close calls, and how lucky the wounded soldiers had been to survive. Now, some of that anxiety returned when I thought about coming home and functioning as a civilian—a husband, a son, and a father. Would I be able to do that? How would I handle my anger about the lies told to us by politicians and the generals? I loved the foot soldiers and admired their bravery, but not the commanders who sent them into combat and talked about favorable body counts.

I had developed a distrust of authority that might make searching for an academic position difficult. I had heard about the demonstrations against the war, the riots, and campus demonstrations. But the *Stars and Stripes* had not gone into details and had minimized the importance of the antiwar marches and demonstrations. Most of the information about rioting and draft-card burning had come to me from listening to Hanoi Hannah, and I thought she must have exaggerated their significance.

RETURN TO GOD'S COUNTRY

We landed at Travis Air Force Base near Sacramento. The wounded soldiers were loaded into several large buses. In Vietnam, heavy metal mesh covered the windows, preventing hand grenades or bombs from being thrown into the buses. These buses had no window screens. The day was cool and dry; the clear blue skies were cloudless. We drove along smoothly to San Francisco. Perhaps Hanoi Hannah had exaggerated the riots and the war protests.

I vaguely recalled, as a youngster, the welcoming people smiling and shouting at the train depot while the train unloaded soldiers returning from World War II. There were congratulation signs and banners, a band playing marches, families embracing soldiers returning from the dangerous fighting. I remember the shouts of joy, the tears, and the kisses. People even crowded the train's open windows to hug soldiers still waiting inside the train. My father emerged from the crowds. Laughing, he lifted me off the ground in an embrace.

But nearing Letterman Hospital, there were crowds of people, mouths open, shouting at our bus and shoving signs at us as we drove slowly past them. They showed a lack of compassion and open hatred toward the wounded soldiers.

Hanoi Hannah had broadcast for months that young Americans were against the war, against the loss of Vietnamese and American lives.

"It's a war just the old people want. They're the only ones who aren't protesting. If you return home, don't expect people to thank you for your service."

I realized she had told the truth about our homecoming.

**

The demonstrators at Letterman's gate held up signs: "Welcome home, child murderers"; "Should have gone to Canada"; "Peace, not war"; "You deserve your wounds." Their angry faces crowded around the bus. Some of us shouted back at the demonstrators. "Cowards, deserters. You don't deserve to live in this country."

The bus windows steamed over. Of course, I resented the peaceniks. Our bus was filled with soldiers who had been sent to fight in place of those who burned draft cards and fled to Canada rather than join the army. I understood their anger, but I was disgusted with the politicians and generals who were directing the war, not the protesters. I worried that the demonstrations encouraged the enemy and caused additional deaths and wounding of our soldiers.

***

The halls of Letterman Hospital looked painfully white to me after a year of living in a camouflage of greens and browns. I wore my sunglasses while following the hospital orderlies pushing Jesse's gurney to the surgical ward. Two surgeons met us in a hallway flooded with unfiltered sunshine. Both wore spotless white uniforms with shiny medals pinned to their shirts. I didn't salute when handing them several envelopes containing Jesse's records.

The truth was that I hadn't felt like a part of the army since my first few months in Vietnam. I no longer saluted. Most physicians I worked with at our evacuation hospital felt the same way. We were there to preserve as many lives as possible. The taking and giving up hills and territory to provoke the enemy and to kill as many of them as possible was a type of stalemated fighting often reported in our newspapers as victories. This was falsely optimistic information. As surgeons, we saw day-to-day serious losses of American soldiers in this war that seemed to be conducted at a distance from both Washington and Hanoi. We were with the army, but not part of the army. I suppose that's one reason we wore clothing that didn't conform with proper military attire in Vietnam, although shorts and sandals were more tolerable in the humid, hot weather, especially when operating gowns added to the overheating.

***

The surgeons at Letterman studied my brief notes about Jesse's operation: the closure of cardiac wounds, closure of the perforated diaphragm, removal of his shattered spleen, resection of part of Jesse's stomach, and closure of multiple bowel perforations. Then they looked at the short incision in Jesse's upper abdomen. They looked again at the operative report.

"How did you perform all those repairs through such a small incision?" one of them asked.

I figured, from that question, they had not experienced combat surgery.

"Jesse's injuries were confined to the upper abdomen and the lower chest, but many different organs were involved. I had a surgical assistant who held up the sternum so I could expose the diaphragm and the pericardium through the abdomen and repair the heart wounds without making a chest incision."

It was better to make an incision longer than necessary than too short and miss an injury because of lack of exposure. As already mentioned, one of my surgical professors used to say, "Small incision, small surgeon."

But it was also not wise to make incisions that were too long, at least longer than necessary. Long incisions took more time to open and to close, and many wounded were waiting for emergency operations. Good judgment about incisions, like everything else, came with experience and careful observations of patients' postoperative courses.

The brightness of the hospital hall had interrupted my thoughts. I pushed the sunglasses more firmly against my face and continued explaining Jesse's surgery to the Letterman physicians.

"The operative report isn't overly descriptive, but it includes the necessary details of all the injuries and repairs. We had large numbers of wounded the night of Jesse's surgery," I added.

"Could you make a diagram of the cardiac surgery?"

With a pencil, I sketched the repair of the heart on Jesse's chart and showed how the sutures closed the cardiac wounds by compressing the heart muscle.

"I'm concerned that the anterior coronary artery might have been narrowed with the repair," I said, "but I felt a normal, vigorous pulse in that artery after the repair, and his EKG shows no sign of cardiac damage or lack of blood supply."

It was late afternoon. I needed to get to the airport to make the last flight home that evening. I shook the surgeons' hands and bent down to Jesse to give him my address and phone number.

"I think you'll be back helping your old man on the farm late this fall, just like you hoped. Any questions, call me."

"Thanks for my life," he answered. I nodded.

I never saw or talked with him again. I was puzzled

that as years passed, I rarely heard from soldiers who had been my patients in Vietnam. Our phone numbers were not hard to find. It was possible to talk with patients, or they could have called me. But I hadn't sought them out. I hadn't even talked with the doctors I had worked with in Vietnam except during hospital reunions.

Perhaps it was because the former patients lived scattered across the States; maybe they had just moved on with their lives, but I thought many must also have had problems with anger and psychological issues and decided not to renew thoughts about the experience of being almost killed in Vietnam. Most of us just wanted to forget about the war and, if possible, make a new start in life. But we were bound together by the war. We had survived at least physically, and back then we never said goodbye.

There was a cab parked near the entrance of the hospital. I told the driver I needed to get to the San Francisco airport as quickly as possible. He answered with a heavy accent, and then drove like a charging Russian Cossack, gripping the steering wheel with white knuckles, shouting at other cars, and motioning with his other arm for everyone to get out of the way. We made it.

There were people ahead of me at the ticket counter having a difficult time choosing their in-flight dinner. Would I miss getting home tonight because people couldn't decide whether they wanted lasagna or beef? Finally, I stepped around them and walked up to the counter.

"I'm just back from Vietnam," I said. "My family will

be waiting tonight to meet me. I don't care about dinner choices—whatever you have will be fine."

The agent probably could smell my wrinkled, soggy uniform.

"There will be a seat for you. We'll hold the flight if necessary," he said.

I was shocked that someone cared about getting me home; they cared about me as an individual and not just as one of a group of people. That hadn't happened for the past year. I ran along the jetway to the airplane. An attendant welcomed me on board.

"There you are," she said. "We were waiting for you."

She grasped my arm and escorted me down the aisle to the front of the plane and a vacant window seat—a large, soft leather seat, so soft I thought it might be broken.

"What would you like to drink?" She smiled. Her blue uniform fit her young, slender form perfectly.

Never knowing when we might be attacked or be called to surgery for emergencies, I hadn't had much alcohol in Vietnam.

"Scotch would be wonderful," I answered, almost as a joke, not expecting anything of that sort. She smiled. Her bright lipstick and white teeth were as shocking as that first drink of alcohol. My God, I was out of touch. Most of my female Vietnamese patients' teeth had been stained dark red or even black from chewing betel nuts.

"Welcome home," she said, handing me the Scotch with a swivel stick, an engraved napkin, and a whiff of her spicy perfume. I caught a glimpse of heaven.

I sipped the alcohol slowly. I thought how different combat surgery had been from my surgical training. In Vietnam, it had sometimes been one operation after another for days, hundreds of patients. And yet, I hadn't known any of the wounded men. They were admitted, rushed to surgery, and then evacuated from Vietnam as soon as possible to make room for more wounded soldiers. I had tried to avoid the gruesomeness of war and the stress caused by listening to details of their combat by limiting time spent in the surgical wards and had returned quickly to the operating rooms. But I missed getting to know many of the wounded and missed many civilian-patient stories I had often listened to during surgical residency. Postoperative surgical care in Vietnam, or I suppose in any war, was depersonalized, almost automatic. If I thought a patient was ready for evacuation from the war, I wrote *Evacuate* in the orders. There was no discussion with anyone else and no deliberation. It was part of our military training. We developed a few close friendships, but it was best not to become dependent; no one was irreplaceable.

***

The steady drone of engines after takeoff helped me sleep most of the way to Iowa until the initial approach for landing. I remember looking out of the aircraft window and being surprised how the Iowa countryside, now dark except for isolated farm lights, blended seamlessly with the black sky and scattered stars. It must have been late in the evening when we landed at the Cedar Rapids airport.

RETURN TO IOWA (SEPTEMBER 1969)

Only a few passengers walked off the plane. I was the only soldier. Except for lighting along the ramps and stairs, the airport was darkened and quiet. The shops, small restaurants, and coffee shops were all shuttered. *Well,* I thought, *at least I've made it home.*

Then I saw them standing in the airport lobby—my family: Mimi, our two children, Steve (now seven) and Mollie (now three), and both sets of parents. They cheered, and Mimi ran toward me with the kids. Steve reached to shake my hand, but I grabbed his shoulders and held him tightly while he hugged my waist. The hugs, kisses, and happy shouting. Mollie ran to her mother and held Mimi's skirt tightly while she looked up at the wrinkled, sunburned stranger everyone was hugging. I reached for her, but she ducked behind her mother. I reached for everybody else and held Mimi tightly. Mollie still wanted her mother to hold her. Mom and Dad seemed about the same. They looked intently at me as if checking for damage, and I looked at them without seeing anything wrong. Mimi's parents looked on and smiled. Perhaps a noisy celebration with other returning soldiers would have been wonderful, but our reunion was personal and, I think, deeply meaningful. We were all thankful and relieved to be together again. It was an excruciatingly happy reunion.

***

Our family came together. We talked about some of the worries and some of our fears of the past year, but not much about the close calls that, for me, were still uncomfortably recent. We bought a car, travelled to amusement parks, had outdoor picnics, enjoyed small get-togethers with friends, and talked late into the nights. I asked Mimi about staying with our parents and watching over our two children while I was overseas. They had stayed, alternating, with each set of grandparents for six weeks. Moving back and forth caused some problems because the parents treated the children differently. A more formal behavior characterized Mimi's parents' home: dinner was at noon; each person at the dinner table was expected to tell what they had done the previous days, or to discuss something of interest to them. In my parents' home, dinner was when Dad arrived from the hospitals, and was often interrupted by medical telephone calls. My father took the children on long walks in the country on weekends and showed them the different ways animals and plants lived in nearby pastures and forests. Mimi's father went flying in his small airplane most Sundays. He offered to take the children with him, but my father had taken care of many injured pilots of small spotter planes in Europe and didn't want the children to fly except in larger, commercial aircraft.

Mimi bridged family differences that year without significant disagreements. I'm not certain exactly how she did it, but she is a careful listener with an excellent memory and a good sense of humor; she's also a natural arbitrator, traits each of our children fortunately absorbed.

"My father and I had a few significant disagreements about how to discipline our children," she told me. "He frequently interrupted the children, telling them to speak up when we sat together at the dinner table talking about whatever might interest them. And Stephen had some eczema on his fingers and sometimes rubbed his hands together, which also bothered my father. There were other things, just little things he said to them, I guess, but I thought the children had enough on their minds with the war and our separation. They needed more kindness and consideration."

"Why didn't you tell me about those times?" I asked her.

"I didn't want to add to your concerns, especially while you were in Vietnam. I thought if you knew about the children being disciplined by my father, you might not want them to visit my parents."

FORT ORD, CALIFORNIA (SEPTEMBER 1969)

I had to adjust to noncombat army surgical practice; putting thoughts of ripping, tearing combat wounds away as best I could and thinking about life after the army, about my family, and civilian surgical practice. I was assigned to the Fort Ord hospital for my final year in the army. Most of the time, I worked in the surgical clinic, seeing one patient after another and dealing with minor surgical problems. Just picked up the next chart in the stack and called out the name. Someone would stand up and be escorted into my office. A few soldiers had worrisome complaints that required careful investigation, but many more had complaints they hoped would keep them out of Vietnam. Some had even swallowed broken razor blades to avoid the war. Very few clinical problems required major surgery. I usually finished the day by early afternoon. The slow pace of surgery, the paper shuffling, and unending administrative directives were intolerable. In Vietnam, I had directed my work and studies without others telling me what to do and when to do it. I had used the relative quiet between major fighting to work at Vietnamese hospitals and to operate on Vietnamese civilians with complicated war wounds at our hospital with Dr. Phouc. But at Fort Ord, time away from the hospital was essentially wonderful, free time. I built a soapbox derby racer with Steve. Mollie liked to sit in it and steer while being pushed. We took the racer to the hills of Fort Ord, and Steve was old enough to steer and apply the brakes. He tore down lots of them, the brakes smoking him to a stop.

The rumble of combat and the cries of the wounded persisted in my mind, like a nightmare following closely behind me. Sleep was interrupted by cries of wounded soldiers and visions of their shredded, bleeding wounds. Thoughts of combat injuries often caught up with me whenever I stopped for rest.

There was a moderate earthquake one night a week after we arrived at Fort Ord in California. I rolled off the bed onto the floor before Mimi was fully awake. I searched for my gas mask, flak vest, and .45 pistol and tried to crawl under the bed, but the mattress was still on the floor without a bed frame. Mimi heard the swearing. She hugged and spoke softly to me until I calmed down. We talked and embraced until dawn. It felt like I had been rescued from combat, even born again because of her love.

I was not the same person who went to war. I thought about the men still serving there and the ones gone forever. Like many Vietnam veterans, I was angry at perceived injustices, and I had a suspicious dislike of people in authority, especially politicians. I worried that sudden, unfiltered anger might cause problems if I didn't take a few moments to think before replying to comments or actions I didn't agree with. Someone might say they thought the war was a mistake. That statement, not specific, didn't bother me much. In fact, I mostly agreed with it. Usually, it was spoken at universities or parties attended by people who hadn't been in the military. I understood their feelings, but not their lack of informed reasoning. I disagreed with the war's conduct, the war's waste, and didn't think the corrupt, unstable South Vietnamese government was worth defending.

But if they kept talking and said something like "I admire those heroes who refused to be drafted and went to Canada," then I almost had to be restrained. These were the times when thinking about the dead and wounded soldiers who had gone to Vietnam in place of those who fled to Canada made my anger surface. Was it right to desert their country when they disagreed with national policies and escape into Canada after taking nourishment and whatever else they could from United States? Serving in a noncombat role would have at least been an honorable alternative.

I thought about what might happen in the future to our son, who was now only seven years old. If at a later age, he disagreed with a war and refused to enter the military, I might agree with his decision. Losing him in combat would have been devastating to me and to our family. I couldn't imagine it.

I also resented the superficial and negative reporting from Vietnam. Most of the correspondents were against the war and reported the agonies and mistakes; they had concentrated on body-count reports while living in Saigon and listening to bar stories night after night instead of witnessing the fighting themselves. What about all the good, brave things? Our medics treated and vaccinated Vietnamese civilians against disease in small towns near Da Nang. Some American doctors lived in Vietnamese cities and worked in the larger civilian hospitals without military protection. Our hospital admitted wounded Vietnamese soldiers and treated them the same as Americans. Many of our hospital admissions were civilians, too badly wounded or too ill for successful treatment anywhere else. Why hadn't correspondents written more about our soldiers helping civilians and the wounded enemy?

DECIDING TYPE OF SURGICAL PRACTICE
AND WHERE TO LIVE (1970)

I had completed four years of medical school, six years
as a surgical resident, and two more as an army surgeon.
Additional training seemed to me to be just indecision
about the future. I had not liked the isolation from patients
when working in research as a resident. Taking care of
patients was, for me, the most educational and enjoyable
choice. I was technically proficient in surgery but hadn't
worked in a research lab for several years. I looked at several good surgical positions available in large clinics and
in academic surgery. Each position might have worked for
us, but there were many faculty members, and advance-
ment to a more responsible position would probably take
years. Also, research and publishing were required in most
surgical centers, and I hadn't spent time in laboratories or
published a surgical paper in several years.

Mimi asked me a question. "You have had so much experience with major trauma. Several hundred cases just
last year. And you have great skill as a clinical surgeon and
enjoy talking with families and patients. Why lose those
abilities by returning to basic research?"

Those thoughts had been on my mind when I looked
at the available surgical positions. Why stand in line when
you could develop your own practice? Why not go to a place
that offered new equipment and new operating rooms and
updated intensive care wards for surgeons who required
them for newer complex specialties?

Mimi and I had both grown up in Iowa. She and the children had stayed there with our parents when I was overseas. The schools were excellent, and Mimi had started working in a commercial real estate firm. There were two large hospitals, and the University of Iowa was only twenty miles away, allowing for convenient exchange of medical information and comparison of different surgical techniques.

In the past, patients with vascular, lung, esophageal, or cardiac problems had been referred either to the university or to the Mayo Clinic. The University of Iowa had developed an ambulance taxi service to transport patients with complicated surgical problems from across the entire state to their surgical department. But, even so, many patients with serious problems were not referred because they declined to leave their homes and travel to the university or other medical centers where the quality of care was uncertain and the physicians were unknown. Many patients with complicated surgical problems never obtained the help they needed.

Funds were available locally to develop these new surgical services at our hospitals, and the medical community was very encouraging. But returning to my boyhood town where my father was still practicing seemed like something a person who had been unsuccessful might do. Like a failure to find elsewhere the support and comfort I had experienced as a boy at home. The move seemed similar to a son returning to take over a small grocery store so his father could retire.

A few months before my army discharge, Mimi and I took a short leave and returned to Cedar Rapids before deciding where we would live and work. One warm autumn afternoon, we looked over downtown from the roof of the highest downtown building, the Merchants' National Bank. Pigeons flew from the flat roof while we looked down at the double-tracked railroad still cutting through the downtown, unchanged from my earliest memories. Several times a day, automobile traffic stopped for a series of boxcars and tankers rolling slowly to and from the world's largest cereal plant, Quaker Oats. Often, dozens of graffiti-covered train cars would almost clear First Avenue, then grind to a stop and reverse direction before the brightly painted cross guards finally rose and cars could cross the tracks. People would sit in their cars, upset by the delays, but comforted somewhat by the odor of cooking oats. Why hadn't something been done to reroute the tracks or the road?

Most of the city's buildings were old brick squares, faded through the years with discolored facades now in need of repair, essentially unchanged from forty-year-old photographs. And a meat-packing factory on the town's edge sent unpleasant odors across parts of town whenever there was a southern wind.

But all possibilities and choices have some disadvantages. That was true in surgery as well as in deciding where we would live and raise our family. Problems can be useful beginnings. Both of us had been away from Iowa for years except the previous year when Mimi and the children had lived with our parents. Neither one of us knew about the new technology and electronic businesses that were bringing many young, energetic people to a town in need of renewal.

When I first started hunting with my father as a young boy, I would stay in the car while Dad went up to a farmhouse to ask for permission to walk their land, looking for pheasants. Very often the farm family would recognize him as the surgeon who had operated on a family member. There would be handshakes and hugs and insistence that we hunt on their farm. The friendliness, even affection, seemed excessive, almost embarrassing to me as a boy. I watched it happen over and over, happy to stay in the car until we started walking through the fields. Even when he had not met the family before, Dad started small talk when people met him in the doorway; they would be pleasant and only asked that we shoot away from the farm buildings and livestock. Perhaps his skill at meeting strangers was honed while walking through rural Wisconsin selling 3D viewers during his college years. It seemed so natural and easy for him to talk to farm families who were receptive and trusting. I remembered this when deciding where to practice medicine. Why not live where people were pleasant?

Mimi and I decided to stay in Iowa.

Rather than joining an academic surgical department and waiting perhaps years for tenure and a full professorship, I drove around central and eastern Iowa to meet family doctors and emergency room physicians. I was amazed how so few doctors cared for so many patients and how so many self-reliant Iowans lived long, happy lives.

Churches and social clubs asked me to talk about my Vietnam surgical experience. I may have still looked young back then, and people may have thought I was inexperienced. So, except in churches where I emphasized our efforts in caring for civilians, I dimmed the lights and projected slides showing the way it really had been: the open chest and abdominal injuries and even wounds involving loss of limbs. At first, the audiences would be silent in the dark auditoriums. Then I could often hear scraping of chairs on wooden floors as people started leaving the room. Once, a person in the audience fainted to the floor. Midway through another slide presentation in dim light, a minister walked through an unseen glass door. I thought those living in peace at home should know what had happened and what was still happening to our soldiers.

I was only thirty-two years old then, but very experienced in trauma and in caring for seriously ill surgical patients. I suppose doctors and patients decided to try out this young MD who had just returned from a war. Maybe spending time talking in hospitals and offices introducing myself to the medical staff helped. For years, I had not paid much attention to the social side of medicine. Working almost constantly, I had little time or energy to form relationships and friendships. I had not properly thanked professors and fellow residents while in training. They had greatly helped me become an effective surgeon. Some had shown me how to discuss the risks and alternatives of surgery and the possible complications of different treatments to the patient and the patient's family. Thinking about those academic friendships as I write this book, I realize it was wrong not to thank all those people.

My father had shown me his bedside manner so many times as I was growing up. He had a natural, relaxed approach and, to the uninformed, could have been part of the patient's family as they discussed the illness and possible treatments. After the war, I finally realized how necessary and important it was to discuss illnesses with the patient and the family. And, unlike combat surgery, the surgeon was not the only physician involved in a patient's care. That's one reason I also tried to meet so many Iowa physicians and administrators after returning home. I should have thanked my father more than I did for showing me his humanistic, concerned approach to patient care.

SURGERY IN IOWA (1969–1998)

My father retired in 1978. I never asked him, but looking back, I think he kept practicing longer than he may have desired with the hope we would return to the Midwest and I would take over his surgical practice. Restless and energetic, he had long enjoyed solo practice without holding meetings to set bylaws or to discuss disagreements. Patient notes during their office visits were handwritten on four-by-six-inch cards. He called the referring doctors to talk about patients they had referred to him. Dictated letters were rare. The office waiting room was always crowded; some patients waiting to see him sat in the next-door pharmacy. The numbers of patients he operated on each year far

exceeded any national average and almost equaled my records from Vietnam. He could sleep instantly and awaken
just as quickly. He was quite frugal in his surgical practice. Remembering the years he had spent walking through
rural Wisconsin selling stereoscopic viewers and boxes of
three-dimensional photographs to pay for his education, I
wasn't surprised to see the molded-plastic waiting-room
chairs, always too few, the minimal handwritten patient
records, several old coagulators he had rewired, and the
single nurse with her assistant who managed the office.

He went hunting in Canada with several doctors each
fall and drove to Florida in the winter to spend a week or
two fishing with some of his retired friends. My mother
worried about him taking so much time away from his surgery. "Clyde, you will lose your patients because of all the
time you take for vacations."

"Well, if that happens, it happens."

But his practice only increased in size, and he didn't
turn down new referrals. "If you do that, people will think
you're quitting," he said.

I talked to him about vascular and thoracic surgery,
and he seemed enthusiastic for the new services, even
knowing it would be different and more complex than his
surgery had been.

"I know things need to change. Just do what's necessary
to develop thoracic and cardiovascular surgery. I know you
will pay attention to the details and do an excellent job."

I think we both were tearful and shook hands in grateful acceptance of his long surgical career and the coming

new generation of surgeons to take care of people in a way he had done for years. That evening, we sat together in Mom and Dad's small family room, sipping Scotch and talking a little, but mostly staring at the bright flames in the fireplace. The decision had been made.

***

The office, already too small, became totally inadequate when my patients arrived in addition to his. I wanted to dictate patients' office visits and send letters to referring doctors. Another nurse, more examining rooms, and at least one transcriptionist were necessary. Office procedures, schedules, even employment contracts needed to be written formally. Office meetings were needed to discuss changes and problems. More space was needed for examination rooms, waiting areas, and for additional doctors' offices. Otherwise, the practice of surgery would remain unchanged, and new specialties couldn't be established.

After Dad retired, I hired another Yale-trained surgeon; we moved to a larger office with more examining rooms, a small procedure room for minor surgery, and more space for future surgeons. A more-formal medical practice was gradually established with written contracts, scheduled office meetings, dictation of office visits, letters to referring physicians, and consultations with office managers and lawyers. More physicians were added to our surgical group to handle the increasing number of referred patients while several of us worked more exclusively in thoracic and vascular surgery.

Dad was a surgeon in charge of one of General Patton's evacuation hospitals for three years in World War II and then performed hundreds of operations over decades of private practice. He continued to assist me and other surgeons in our corporation for several more years until his second heart attack in 1974. His recovery was uncomplicated, but, after hospital discharge, he looked tired and fragile to me, and his color was slightly gray. He and Mom then chose to live out of town in the Iowa countryside near Dad's boyhood home. He seldom complained about anything and went on long walks with Mom, his grandchildren, and his neighbors. I understood his thoughts about the increasing complexity of the surgical practice. There were so many new procedures, so many new subspecialties. But I was worried every day that he would have more problems with his heart, worried that he would slip into progressive heart failure with progressive shortness of breath, or not return from one of his walks along Buffalo Creek, where he had fished and hunted as a young man.

**

I could practice as I had been trained and maintain a narrow focus, but medical knowledge was expanding rapidly, doubling every seven years even before computers and computerization of medical records. There was no doubt that to offer competent, modern services, we had to either contract or expand the practice. Expansion did involve some compromises. When I first began private practice in Iowa, I would leave notes listing things I needed personnel and nurses to accomplish. Communication was informal. This method evolved into a formal system with office and physician meetings each month after hiring physicians, more staff, and constructing our own office building.

Physicians would vote at the meetings about how to proceed with office policies, hiring, contracts, expenses, and discuss problems as they presented. Sometimes I was on the losing side of the vote. This was difficult, especially at first, because I had made most decisions myself in operating rooms in the army and at the beginning of private practice. Also, my debating skills were not the best. But as for staying small or getting more complex, I had made that decision and lived with it.

When I first began working in Iowa as a surgeon, most of my patients came from emergency rooms. One of my first patients was an elderly woman with a chest injury from an automobile accident. She had emphysema and osteoporosis, not a great combination. Several ribs had fractured, and sharp rib fragments had punctured one of her lungs, causing it to collapse. She was gasping for breath and was started on oxygen. There were no breath sounds over the injured chest, and her color was dingy blue. The X-ray showed a completely collapsed lung, and her heart was pushed toward the other side of her chest. I inserted a small tube into the upper part of the injured chest and sat her up on the stretcher. Her breathing became easier as air, under tension, bubbled rapidly from her chest. A second chest X-ray after the tube insertion showed both lungs expanded and normal findings except for the rib fractures. Her physical examination otherwise was normal for her age and fragility. She was admitted for observation to the intensive care unit. The punctured lung healed rapidly and no longer leaked air. She stayed in the hospital about four days, as I remember. Sometimes we talked about the past when I visited her. She lived just a few houses away from my parents!

"Oh, I remember you," she said one day. "You and a cute blond girl used to play in our backyard sandbox. All the little roads and houses, the hills and valleys; you kept adding a little water so the sand could be shaped and not just fall down. You both wanted to marry each other. Can you believe that? I answered that when you both got older, you would meet many other people."

I looked at her wrinkled and smiling face as we talked. I had been certain back then she was wrong. Shaping sand into small villages, adding bits of evergreen for trees, we were in love and would one day marry. But the dreams that little girl and I shared were only dreams. Now that former sandbox playmate lives thousands of miles away.

Two other patients I remember from the early-practice days had been driving an automobile too rapidly on a country gravel road, missed a curve, rolled into a ditch, and smashed through a farm fence. The call came from one of the emergency rooms about two o'clock in the morning. On examination, the driver, a drunken young man, had no pulse in his right leg, and a large fence post was impaled in his upper thigh. The lower leg was cool, cyanotic, pulse-less, and without sensation to pinprick. The young woman, also appearing drunk, had moderate pain in her abdomen and a small laceration just above her umbilicus. Both pa-tients had stable vital signs, but of course I operated on the boy first because of the lack of blood supply to his leg. The wound contained pieces of wood and was covered with dirt. It was very similar to many wounds I had treated in Vietnam. After thorough cleansing of the injury, I replaced the artery with a section of vein rather than a Dacron tube that could more easily become infected than a vein graft. The leg became pink with a new blood supply and, after he awoke, the sensation of his leg had returned to normal.

The girl's injury, just a small cut in the upper abdomen, didn't look as serious, but after cleansing it with alcohol, I could easily pass a sterile hemostat through the wound into her abdomen. She was taken to surgery. After the an-esthetic, her wound was carefully cleaned. I enlarged the wound, searched inside her abdomen and found no in-juries, but could feel a hard, round object just below her liver—a gearshift knob from their crashed pickup. I sent it to pathology as a specimen. After several days, the report returned: "Gearshift knob from 1965 Ford pickup."

Ok, the pathologist was probably correct. He had re-searched the knob and had a good sense of humor.

I was thankful to be fully involved in a clinical practice. There was little free time to think about war. Fatigue kept most of my nightmares of combat injuries at bay. Memories of Vietnam soldiers and their wounds remained, for the most part, subconscious except for nighttime telephone calls from emergency rooms. These calls were like an electric shock that ignited old memories. I would be instantly awake, pull on a pair of scrubs, and quickly drive to the hospital, thinking of those Vietnam soldiers, the ones with missing arms or legs, the ones with uncontrolled bleeding, and hoping the new patient in the emergency room wasn't too severely injured.

One of these patients I was called to see soon after I began surgical practice in Iowa was a young boy who had suffered a gunshot wound. I was at a hardware store looking for parts to rebuild several of our leaky faucets. Our younger daughter, Susan (I think she was just three years old then), and I were looking at rubber washers and new faucet valves. I was showing her how faucets turned on and off when my beeper rang, asking me to call an emergency room. The ER doctor asked me to come immediately. A twelve-year-old boy had accidently discharged his shotgun while climbing over a barbwire fence and had suffered a massive abdominal injury. I drove rapidly to the hospital. Nurses took care of our Susan until Mimi arrived to take her home.

The boy had a severe injury. An X-ray taken before I arrived showed large numbers of metallic shots in his upper abdomen. I learned years later there are about one hundred BBs in the shotgun shells the boy was using to hunt pheasants that day. I never counted them, but thinking now of that X-ray, I realize there could have been one hundred lead BBs scattered inside his abdomen. The boy, pale and sweaty, with a low blood pressure, was taken rapidly to surgery after starting blood transfusions. There were dozens of holes in his small and large bowel, his liver, his spleen, and even his pancreas. There were so many perforations, I lost count. Air was introduced into the stomach to search for more undetected holes. A bloody froth came from several more perforations. They were sutured closed. Part of the boy's colon was removed, and a colostomy was constructed. Drains were placed near the liver and pancreatic injuries. The common duct that normally carried bile from the liver to the intestine had been torn and shattered. It was reconstructed over a rubber T tube.

Several days after his injury, the boy had uncontrollable bleeding from a gastric stress ulcer, requiring removal of part of his stomach. A few weeks later, he had an infection under his left diaphragm that was drained without surgery using fluoroscopic guidance. His recovery was long and interrupted by these and other complications. For weeks, he said he wanted a Mountain Dew but could be given only intravenous feedings until his bowel began to function. Then the day arrived: the family, the nurses, and I watched the boy take his first drink of Mountain Dew, and he then began to take more fluids by mouth. We all had become part of his family. He improved rapidly. I saw him repeatedly in the office. Months later, an X-ray of his common bile duct was obtained. Except for the rubber tube, it looked normal. Finally, the tube was removed, and after several more office visits, he resumed his life.

Months, even years passed. I thought less about his injuries and about all the people involved in his care. Family news of his good health continued for a decade. Then he visited my office with some papers he wanted me to sign. Unrecognizable, he was a muscular, confident young man. Looking carefully at me, he handed over some papers from a notebook.

"I want to join the marines," he said. "The sergeant said I needed to be cleared medically."

I thought of all his altered anatomy, all the rearranging inside his abdomen. Repairing another injury would be difficult or impossible.

I wrote that on his papers, after discussing his long-ago injuries with him and his family. His parents may have been pleased, but he looked disappointed when he put the note from the marine recruiter back into his briefcase. Then, I lost contact with him for decades until his family sent me his obituary. He had died from a rare malignancy of the common duct that drained bile from his liver! Could it have been caused by the long-ago injury and the rubber tube that had been in place while his own duct healed? I was heartbroken for his family and for all the people who had worked so hard to enable his survival from the hunting accident decades before. I am still heartbroken when I think about how brave he was, and can still see his father and mother worried and wide-eyed, waiting for me on those dark mornings in the hallway outside the intensive care unit to ask about their son.

***

Surgery can be uplifting; often difficult operations save patients, and you feel great then, like a king. But sometimes there are major postoperative difficulties despite the best plans and an operation that technically was without problems. Sometimes surgical care is modified after careful thought about these cases, but often nothing can be found different from similar cases without postoperative complications. You may never know. But you can't have it both ways; you can't compare different treatments in the same patient. You gather available information, make a choice for treatment, plan it, then do it as carefully as possible and face the consequences, good or occasionally bad. As my professor in thoracic surgery used to say, "Don't try to screw the unscrewable."

I believe that's true, but often in emergencies or in combat surgery, many situations require rapid improvisation without chances for planning the night before or at any other time before the procedure. At the start of that type of surgery, there is often little information about the exact injuries, and the patients are too unstable to allow diagnostic procedures.

***

Working as a surgeon in Iowa, I would meet the family and the patient the evening before scheduled surgery. Most families gathered to support not only the patient, but also their doctors. All questions and possible surgical outcomes needed to be discussed. Careful discussions with the patient and families were key to everyone's understanding. Sometimes a complete recovery from a patient's preoperative illness wasn't possible. Still, surgery might offer hope for improvement in comfort or function. Patients were usually grateful and wanted to resume their work as soon as possible.

"When can I get back to work?"

That was often one of their first questions.

***

After a solo practice of vascular and thoracic surgery for three years, the need to develop heart surgery became more urgent. Several excellent cardiologists had begun practice in our city and were interested in the development of a cardiac surgical program. The care of these patients was not optimal without high-quality cardiac surgery available near their homes.

Coronary artery bypass had not yet been performed when I was a resident. It was necessary for me to take a leave of absence to learn the latest techniques. A recently trained cardiac surgeon from Yale joined our group. The monitoring of surgical patients was updated in the intensive care ward, and an operating room was equipped with advanced electronics and duplication of the electrical supply. Two open-heart machines were installed, and technicians were hired to run them. We ran test after test to coordinate operative procedures and performed several open-heart operations on dogs until we were satisfied that all the equipment was operating without problems.

A funny thing: our first cardiac surgical patient was referred to us by a veterinarian who had watched us operate on dogs while we were checking all the equipment necessary for human open-heart surgery. One of his close friends developed angina; his angiogram showed severe narrowing of the coronary arteries.

"Why don't you have these surgeons bypass those arteries?" he said to his friend. "I've watched them operate on my dogs, and they did a great job."

The surgical team had excellent results. The number of patients soon increased dramatically. Additional surgeons were hired, and two new surgical rooms were constructed exclusively for open-heart surgery. The cardiac surgeons on our team travelled to surgical centers to determine whether newly published techniques were useful and safe before adopting them. When necessary, we operated on animals in research laboratories using the most recently developed techniques and instruments as part of the evaluation.

Usually, these modifications promised more-durable surgical outcomes, such as repair of the mitral valve rather than replacing it, enabling some patients to avoid long-term use of blood thinners. The use of arteries in the chest wall for more-durable bypass of diseased coronary arteries became standard practice.

***

Several years after our surgical team started performing open-heart surgery, my father began having progressively severe chest pain with exertion. There had been times recently when he would suddenly stop walking, his face turning pale with perspiration beading his forehead, sometimes grasping his left arm and shoulder.

"What's wrong, Dad?" As if I didn't know.

"Nothing, just resting for a minute."

I was worried he might not have enough heart muscle left to avoid heart failure or that he would suffer dangerous arrhythmias or even experience sudden death. We didn't talk about these possibilities. He knew about them as well as I did, and I thought talking about them might cause more anxiety for him. He finally agreed to undergo cardiac catheterization.

The coronary arteriogram showed severe three-vessel coronary artery disease and compromise of his left ventricular function, not surprising findings considering his previous heart attacks. Coronary bypass was recommended as the best treatment even though it would be risky because of his heart damage. Our open-heart surgical teams were now well organized and well experienced; each of the two teams operated many times each week with very few problems.

My mother told me that Dad refused to go elsewhere for his surgery. A few days later, I stopped by their home to talk to them both about the risks and hopeful results of coronary bypass. I was anxious about performing his surgery because of his age and because the previous two serious heart attacks made him a high risk. And, most of all, because he was my father. I had hoped he had changed his mind and would go elsewhere for his surgery. What if he didn't do well with surgery? Would he be strong enough to survive possible serious complications? And what if he didn't survive surgery? If these things happened, the surgical team and I would be severely depressed. Days before his operation, sleep became difficult. I had recurrent nightmares about possible complications relating to his operation, even his death. If he had chosen to travel elsewhere for surgery, complications, even his death, might have been easier for me and for the family to bear.

But he asked me to be his surgeon. I stopped offering alternatives and listened quietly.

This is what I remember about his illness:

The small blue hospital room smelled of antiseptics and rubbing alcohol. My seventy-nine-year-old father lay in a shiny metal bed, barely outlined beneath white sheets glaring in the late-afternoon sun. He refused to leave his hometown to have coronary bypass surgery. He wanted me, his son, to perform the operation. Surgery was scheduled for the following day.

"Dad, I'll take you anywhere. The Mayo Clinic. I know several cardiac surgeons in Cleveland. Remember, I almost joined them? I'll take you back to Yale."

"No, no. Your mother is ill. You know how dizzy she gets when stressed, even disoriented. She likes our place up on the farm and wouldn't do well if we went anywhere else for an operation. Besides, I know your team well, and you have a good record. I'll either have surgery here or live as long as possible without it."

There was an open, yellow-edged, wrinkled Bible on his bedside table, the one Dad had carried through the war in France and the battle for Bastogne. A thin red ribbon marked psalm twenty-three. I had seen that psalm of David in Vietnam, where some marines had shortened tattooed versions on their arms: *I fear no evil for you are with me.* Or a variant used by the Special Forces: *I fear no evil for I am the meanest motherfucker in the valley.* The soldiers with those tattoos belonged to a fraternity of men involved in high-risk combat. Perhaps the tattoos pushed away fright and encouraged the soldiers to be brave. But I realized the only time I saw that tattoo was on the chest or arms of wounded soldiers. Those imprinted words hadn't been very helpful.

As combat surgeons in war, both my father and I had doubts that God looked after individuals or either army. The wounded all belonged to a desperate fraternity, bonded by more than the color of uniforms or tattoos. We hoped that God looked after all of them.

But I had never seen Dad get into bed without kneeling in prayer. So what was his faith? What did he think or say when kneeling at his bedside? I wished I had asked him, but I doubt he would have discussed anything so personal. Perhaps a simple *Thank you, God* for survival. That's a prayer I had said after near misses in Vietnam. And I had asked for guidance when faced with grievous soldier wounds. But, embarrassed that someone might hear, I had prayed silently. I never knelt or asked for help out loud. No one could tell I was praying, but when rockets fell nearby or a soldier was close to death unless his hemorrhaging was immediately stopped, I had prayed for guidance. Still, I suppose Dad was more brave. He openly knelt and prayed softly whenever he thought it was necessary. But if there was a God, I thought he would get the prayer whether it was spoken or sincerely thought. I usually just prayed when faced with severe danger, when prayers were more easily thought of than spoken.

On evening rounds, I stopped by his room again. We talked casually about going hunting when he recovered. My muscles relaxed as I sat beside his bed and thought beyond tomorrow. Weekends, we had often gone hunting together—whatever was in season. After Clyde's father died, his family depended on him and his two brothers to provide food by fishing and hunting. Clyde had long used a double-barreled shotgun with just two shots.

"Why would I need more than that? After shooting twice, nothing is in range anymore." I preferred a modern five-shot automatic after seeing pheasants fly away while reloading a two-shot gun.

Surgery was set for tomorrow morning.

I was about to leave his room when he motioned me closer. "You want a little Scotch before you leave?" he said, reaching under the Bible for a thin silver flask. Smiling, I walked to the bedside, resting my hand on the cool bedrail.

"I knew you must have it hidden somewhere in here." I closed the door and opened one of the windows, then poured a finger of Scotch into two paper cups and sat down near the bed. That evening I was off-call.

"Here's to you, Dad."

"Here's to both of us, and here's to tomorrow," Clyde answered, laughing softly. The straight alcohol burned.

I walked to the window; it was cold and dark, early evening. I turned back to my father, now more serious.

"Why were you so hard on me when I was growing up?"

"I don't remember being hard—maybe just trying to make you see the value of work and not giving up."

If he had shown a little love with all the teaching, it would have helped. After all, I wasn't born tough.

"Remember when you left for the war? I was nine years old. You were getting on the train. You put down your duffel bag and shook my hand. 'Keep things running as they should,' you said."

"You weren't still in short pants; I thought it was a good thing to say."

"Was that what most fathers would have done?"

"What do I care what most fathers would have done? I was talking to you."

"I tried to be in charge just like you said. I opened the packages you sent before Mom got home from work. The German helmets, gas masks, the Luger and Mauser rifle, that German flag covered with blood. Later she would see what you had sent and hide them somewhere in the basement. She and Grandma read your letters in whispers and then put them away too. I was frightened. The news on the radio was not good. That was about the time your hospital was captured. I thought you would never come home. Mom was frightened too. I thought I wasn't doing a good job taking care of anyone, like you had asked me to do. Like I had failed. A few years later, you doubted I'd make the honor society."

I remembered that Dad thought my grades needed improvement and that I wasn't as strong a wrestler as some of the farm boys on other teams. But I had made it to the state finals even though he might have been surprised. I also remembered he thought surgical training might be too demanding for me.

It was as if he were a blacksmith hammering his still-impressionable son into hardness.

But now wasn't the time for us to talk about these things even though I had accepted some of his thoughts as if they were advice, and many of them seemed to meddle in my life. Then we were silent for a few minutes.

"Well, maybe it wasn't all kisses and hugs. Sometimes I was just wrong. But it worked; didn't it? I mean, you did just fine."

"Was it five years ago I shot you in Canada?" I said.

"Seven years."

"Just two small lead shots. You were on the other side of that small lake. The wind must have carried them."

"Well, they hit me in the head hard enough to break through the skin." Clyde reached up to his right temple. "Here, feel them."

"I don't have to feel them; you tell the story and show those small lumps to almost everyone. It's embarrassing. Let me take them out tomorrow."

"Hell no. I won't sign the op permit for that."

"Well, keep them. Just try not to tell the story so often. I only shot you once in thirty years. That isn't too bad, I guess."

I thought that it may have been unwise to bring these past events up, especially the night before his surgery. After all, we both needed to be ready for the trials of tomorrow. In preparation, we should have been calm, but our emotions were still swinging back and forth.

Clyde straightened his pillow; we both laughed again.

Silence, then a few tears. We both smiled and held hands for a moment. I touched his head softly and got up to leave.

"See you tomorrow. Don't worry. We have the best team. I could do it with my eyes closed, but I'll keep them open tomorrow."

"I raised you to not do a half-assed job no matter what the hell you were working on. Funny, though, I never thought about me being *the job* you would be doing. And me asleep, not keeping an eye on things."

"Sure, Dad, sure. But those days are over. Relax. Now we will look after you."

Walking away from his room, along the darkened hall, I thought, *Why the hell didn't you just go somewhere else? Do you know how hard this will be on the team if you don't make it? On Mom? On me?* How had I allowed this to happen? Why had I chosen to become a cardiac surgeon instead of choosing a more sane specialty like dermatology?

***

There were two different ways to reach the hospital's operating rooms. One was just a straight walk from the parking lot down a hallway and then up some stairs. There were a few bulletin boards on the walls announcing various meetings and hospital events in addition to lists of recent contributors to the hospital, but nothing unexpected, unusual, or inspiring. That was the hallway I usually used each morning. The other hallway to the surgical floor passed by the chaplain's office. On the opposite wall, there was a large painting of Jesus with his arms extended as if reaching to his disciples. Jesus appeared to be looking at me, his arms beckoning. His face and gesture settled me and somehow indicated I would not be facing the day's problems alone. The oil painting had a settling effect, a calmness I had experienced in European cathedrals. I would stop for a few moments to look at him and his arms reaching toward me. I could then think the problems I faced were only part of more-important and greater troubles than mine. I'll admit I walked this route on mornings when I faced serious problems or when difficult surgery was scheduled—like today. No one else was in the hallway. There were no lights in the chaplain's office. Still, my thoughts and simple prayers were silent.

I prayed when in need or when in danger. But my

words of prayer were silent and seemed shallow compared to Dad's approach to prayer and very cursory compared to Father Perez's tending to all of us in Vietnam. I could see Perez kneeling over wounded soldiers and praying out loud, without apology, hands together, uniform and vestments sweat-soaked.

Still, I prayed when seriously threatened. Praying granted quiet moments of calmness, a sharing of concern about future choices and, sometimes, eased guilt about past surgical complications even though they might have been unavoidable.

***

I stood at the window of the operating room, watching Dad being moved onto the surgical table. Nurses were organizing instruments, and technicians were readying the heart-lung machine for the coronary artery bypass operation. His chest was painted with iodine; sterile blue drapes were then applied with a narrow, vertical window over the sternum. I adjusted my headlight and magnifying eye lenses, scrubbed my hands and arms, and soon was dressed in a sterile gown and gloves.

The anesthetist wrote on a clipboard; nurses finished organizing the surgical instruments. Technicians completed loading saline into the heart-lung machine. Standing at the right side of the operating table with an assistant opposite me, I still felt alone even though the team had worked together for several years. I stared at Clyde's white skin, illuminated by two powerful overhead lights. *Just like all the others,* I thought, trying to take one careful step at a time and hoping to take away the emotional weight pulling against every move. *One step at a time.*

"Knife!"

Diane placed it perfectly into my outstretched hand. I cut through the skin.

"Saw!"

I opened the sternum, almost automatically after seven hundred heart operations. The heart was exposed.

"Take it away and cool five degrees."

The heart-lung pump whined into action; darkened, desaturated blood flowed to the machine through plastic tubes, then was mixed with oxygen and pumped back into Clyde's body through more tubes. I was surrounded by tubes of his rapidly flowing blood. The heart emptied and stopped beating, fibrillating and cold to the touch. I held up the heart apex to look at the back side and saw a large gray scar and muscle loss; even the front wall of the ventricle hadn't contracted normally before it fibrillated. Perhaps the heart was too badly damaged to be helped. My mouth became dry. My father's voice echoed:

"You can't stop now. That would leave me where I was; I would die. Go ahead; do the operation; I'd rather take my chances with surgery."

I felt the ropy hardness of the calcified coronary arteries along the surface of the heart. There were some soft sections of these arteries that felt almost normal. These areas would be used for the bypass grafts to deliver blood around the damaged vessels. Another surgeon took veins from one of Dad's legs to use as bypass conduits. Clyde's body was now five degrees cooler than normal to decrease the amount of oxygen needed for metabolism. The cold aorta was clamped just above the heart and the heart stopped with potassium solution. My hands absorbed the cold, becoming almost numb. I thought to myself, *Be accurate, but be quick. Longer times on the heart-lung pump increase the risk.*

The lower ends of the bypass grafts were sewn to the selected coronary arteries. The other ends of the vein grafts were sewn to the aorta. Five grafts in all. Blood was then allowed to flow down the bypass grafts to the heart muscle.

I turned to the technicians who controlled the temperature of the blood circulating through the machine.

"Rewarm."

I gave the heart a few minutes to receive the blood through the bypass grafts and allow it to rewarm to strengthen its contractions. Besides the whine of the heart-lung machine, the room was quiet. None of the usual soft music. No one was talking. None of the usual jokes. No one came into or out of the room to minimize exposure to airborne bacteria.

I relaxed for a moment and thought about hunting with my dad:

There is a boy of thirteen trudging into the searing wind along a snowy ditch; his father walks the graveled road beside him. The youngster scuffs open rabbit burrows; long streams of loosened snow blow away behind them. His leather boots, first soaked with slush, now frozen and cutting his ankles. A few tears frozen on his skin, his fingers are senseless. After three miles he hears his father:

"Are you ready to turn back to the truck?" The boy looks up at his father: the snow-caked brows and lashes, the narrow streaks of ice across his face. But Clyde still smiles slightly, his lips fastened around a glowing red cigarette. He must be hurting too, *the boy thinks.*

"Let's go on a while, Dad," he says. "We only have three rabbits so far."

He wants to pound his father into submission, into the gravel, to admit pain and exhaustion, to admit his son is tougher. A rabbit suddenly runs ahead. They both raise their guns, but the boy is quicker and shoots first. Now they have four. They walk silently into the red sunset back to the truck.

"Sir, I think the patient is warm enough to come off the bypass machine now."

It was one of the pump technicians. The anesthesiologist gave intravenous medications to strengthen the heart contractions. The heart-lung machine then gradually pumped less blood as the heart, with its new bypasses, took over. The blood pressure first was 120, then after less than a minute, the pressure began to fall—110, 100, 80. The heart became dilated.

I turned to the pump technicians.

"Take it away again."

Damnit, I thought. *Is the scarred heart strong enough to*

take over on its own? It's just what I feared might happen.
We let the heart rest on bypass for a while and mixed more
potent medicines to stimulate the heart. Still, on the next
try to gradually stop the heart-lung machine, the heart
again failed to support an adequate blood pressure, and the
machine had to be restarted.

"Rewarm another degree. Concentrate the medications
before we try to come off the bypass machine again."

Dry-mouthed, I turned to the pump technicians. "We
may have to use a balloon in the aorta to maintain blood
pressure after surgery."

"The balloon and the pump to drive it are in the room,
sir," one of them said.

I looked at the clock. Surgery had started three hours
ago. The operation was taking too long. My relatives, sister,
and mother would know there was a problem. Using the
intercom, I asked a nurse at the surgical department desk
to talk to my family in the waiting room and explain the
situation.

I looked at the technicians. "Let's try to come off the
bypass machine again now." The concentrated medications
were started.

"Three-quarters flow," I asked.

The machine slowed its pumping. The blood pressure
was 80.

"Increase the medications. Half flow." The pressure
stayed the same. "One-quarter flow." The machine slowed
more.

"Pump off," I said.

After a minute, the whine stopped. The blood pressure remained borderline at 80. "Transfuse 100 cc." The pressure was now 90.

"Another 100 cc." The blood pressure rose to 110. The damaged heart required careful stretching with transfusions. Too much stretching would damage the muscle, and the heart would fail to pump adequately.

"Transfuse another hundred. No, take off fifty." A minute later: "Now add fifty." It was like walking a tightrope, leaning first to one side, then to the other. After another half hour, the blood pressure became more stable.

"Let's have a little music," I said, removing the plastic tubes from the heart. The blood thinner was neutralized. Some of the medications were able to be slowed. Hank Williams sang softly.

I stayed with Clyde as he was taken to the intensive care unit and sat at the monitor console for several hours, carefully manipulating the medications and transfusions. Bleeding from the chest tubes slowed as his temperature rose to normal and his heart became stronger with the new blood supply.

Finally, I walked to the surgical waiting room. Mom, a handkerchief in her hand and brushing away tears, walked quickly to me. She put her arm around my waist; there were hugs and kisses.

"We've been so worried. It took such a long time. You must be exhausted, dear. Thank you, thank you."

I embraced Mom and my sister. "We had some problems because of his heart attacks and loss of muscle. But he's doing well now."

I felt like a survivor myself, like a patient who had survived a critical illness.

"Oh, Bill, he wouldn't go anywhere else. After helping you with surgery the past few years, he said there was no one with better judgment or a finer pair of hands. He wanted you to be his surgeon."

He had never told me what he thought about my surgical techniques or judgments, but we had sometimes operated together on patients with serious vascular emergencies and even major liver resections.

Removing his gown and gloves after we had finished those operations, he might have said, *Well, that was interesting. I thought you handled that problem quite well.*

***

Two days after surgery, Clyde continued to improve and was transferred from the intensive care unit to a surgical ward. The next morning, he was found walking the halls, disoriented. I arrived quickly. He was walking rapidly along a corridor, uncombed gray hair all angles, unshaven, no robe, his rear hanging out of the medical gown.

"Dad, what's going on?"

"I had dreams last night. Did you know everything is good?" he said. "There are no bad things, just shades of good. Even when you're sleeping, you dream happy endings." Eyes wide open, he shouted, "I need to tell everybody!" and wandered down the hall. Nurses found an old box of Quaaludes near the Scotch in his room. Two pills were missing.

"Well, hell, I didn't want to disturb anybody. They were busy all night long, so I didn't ask them for a sleeper. Just took my own."

We helped him back to bed; then I leaned close to Dad's face.

"That medicine you took can cause disorientation, even depress your heart. I expect you to help yourself get well, damnit; don't be part of the problem."

Arms restrained, he stared at the ceiling for a few hours until the effect of the Quaaludes was gone.

***

Four weeks after surgery, my office phone rang. "Hello, Doc. This here is Donny. You know, I live on the farm across the road from your dad. I don't want to bother you; don't want to tattle on old Doc, but I thought you ought to know. Yesterday morning, just about light, I looked out my south window and seen him crawling GI-style through the snow and hay stubble pushing his shotgun ahead of him. He was goin' toward the lake. Well, after he crawled about fifty yards, he suddenly stands up. Three Canadian geese take off from the lake, and he gets two of them. He invites me over for supper. They tasted damn good, but is he supposed to be doing that much?"

The next month, Dad called the office, the first time we had spoken in several weeks. Country music was playing softly. I turned up the radio volume, knowing it would irritate him, and then spoke into the phone.

"How's it going, Dad?"

"What's all that racket? Can you hear me?"

"Sure, Dad."

"Just wanted to tell you that it's cold as hell up here on the farm, and the wind's blowing hard. The lake froze over. I decided to go ice-skating. Walked through the snow to the lake, put the skates on, and skated as hard as I could into the wind to the other side. No chest pain. I guess you must not have made too many mistakes.

"Come up when you can, and we'll have a whiskey."

TIME WITH FAMILY AND FRIENDS, IOWA, HAITI (1969–1998)

Dad lived on for thirteen additional years. We often visited him and Mom with our children. Dad continued to take them on long walks whatever the season. He taught them much about nature, much about the plants and animals. Now, as adults, they still talk about those walks. Not only about what they learned from their grandpa, but especially how long the walks were despite the intense heat of summers or the brittle coldness of Iowa winters. I think he also wanted to instill toughness in them, something they would need later in life. For the most part, I think he had an enjoyable time, but it wasn't all pleasant. Mom had progressive cognitive dysfunction. Dad did his best to care for her but became exhausted. Caring for her, I think, caused him more isolation from his friends, who also became progressively more disabled with advancing age. But he stubbornly maintained a physical and mental toughness that seemed to help him make new friends with people living nearby his country home. He and his neighbor, Donny, walked the Iowa countryside. They planted many trees on land unsuited for farming. Dad must have shown Donny how to look for four-leaf clovers and perhaps how to hunt and fish. Donny taught Dad how to repair machines. One favorite of mine was a four-wheel-drive vehicle Donny welded together in his machine shed. Despite the cold winter weather, they liked to drive it along the frozen Buffalo Creek, purposely sliding wildly and trying to form perfect tricks like figure eights and circles on the ice. They would take grandchildren on rides and afterward build bonfires on the ice to roast hot dogs and marshmallows.

But, unlike Donny, Dad never did much preventive maintenance.

One February, he called me about his snowblower. "I can't get the blower to start. One of the tire chains came off."

It had snowed the night before and now was near zero. The snowblower was in an unheated garage. A tire chain had come off and been drawn up into the reel that gathered snow into the front of the machine. Wearing insulated jackets, leather gloves, and cleated shoes, we both pulled on the chain and couldn't get it free.

"Oh, let's just forget it," Dad said. "We can shovel the driveway, and I'll call someone to pick up the snowblower and service it next week."

"I know you haven't ever changed the oil or serviced it, but the chain just came off and got thrown into the machine," I said. "We should be able to fix it."

Frosted breath fogged our glasses and clouded our vision. Wrenches were rusted and old, but one was still adjustable and fit.

I loosened several bolts that held the reel to the rest of the machine. We both pulled hard again—one of us in his fifties, the other somewhere past eighty. Steam poured out of our mouths and noses from all the exertion. Dad wouldn't stop to rest. Neither would I. It was more of the unending competition we shared since I was a young boy. There were arguments about how we could get the chain free and what tools to use. We both pulled at the chain, but it stayed caught between the reel and the body of the blower.

"This isn't working," he said. "I'll pull the damn chain while you hold the snowblower steady."

"Why not rope it to the garage so we can pull together in the same direction?" I said.

A whistling wind blew sheets of snow around edges of the garage door.

Dad continued looking down at the cement floor.

"No, you just hold the machine; I'll pull on the damn chain. On three," he said. "One, two, three, pull!"

Suddenly the chain came flying free. Soaked with

sweat, we both skidded away in different directions on a layer of ice. Covered with grease, we sat laughing on the floor, thankful that no one had seen two surgeons banging and pulling on that old snowblower.

"Dad, you need to keep the tires inflated. Nothing's broken. The chain just slipped off because the tire was flat."

"That may have been what happened," he said. "But maybe not."

"Maybe yes. Got any other explanations?"

We cleaned the frost off our glasses, tightened the bolts, put some air in the tires, and blew off the driveway.

Then we had several weekend shots of Glenlivet.

***

The next decade passed quickly. The children were getting older now and wondered exactly what I did as a doctor, as a surgeon. As my father had taken me, I sometimes took them with me to emergency rooms and surgical rounds on weekends. I continued to go on medical missions to Haiti and started taking each of our children, when they became teenagers, on trips to the Albert Schweitzer Hospital in Haiti, where they watched doctors in the operating room, saw patients in the surgical clinic, and sometimes assisted me in surgery. During the Haitian mission with our daughter Mollie, we were asked to examine a young woman with a painful, distended abdomen and severe anemia. She needed urgent surgery. Mollie assisted me that day. We opened the abdomen and suctioned away a large amount of blood. There was an ectopic, bleeding pregnancy attached to the patient's left ovarian tube. We removed it and stopped the bleeding. The scrub nurse looked at the fetus. "Oh, so sorry," she said. "It's a boy." Mollie, now a professor in neurobiology, still shakes her head when she remembers that day.

***

Dad was doing well and continued to live near the small Iowa town of Winthrop. Thoughts about Vietnam and all the casualties became less frequent. A few of my friends had fought in Vietnam, but as the years passed, we seldom talked about combat or the war anymore. If people asked me how I felt about the war and what I had experienced in Vietnam, I usually changed the subject; most of those who asked had no idea of the horrors soldiers had suffered and how relating those experiences from decades ago still caused nighttime revisiting of bodies and blood. I had hoped to someday write about combat surgery, but had avoided most of the stories told by wounded soldiers when I was in Vietnam because they had just happened, and the grisly immediacy of details and the anxiety of soldiers telling them were infectious and disrupted my work as a surgeon.

I attended the annual reunions of the 95th Evacuation Hospital for a few years, but most of the people who attended were in Da Nang after I had left the combat zone, because the hospital had remained active for years after I

had served there. A few former Vietnam soldiers were still
close friends. I was able to talk with them about wartime
experiences because we shared life-threatening situations
and had lost close friends in Vietnam. It was a sharing of
emotions and memories still painful despite the intervening years. And open questions such as *How did you feel
about all the killing?* or *How could you have seen all those
wounded and dead soldiers and hope to ever find peace?*
were not asked. Our stories had happened long ago, and
the intervening years had blurred enough details so they
almost seemed to have happened to someone else. Many
had been in combat and told distinctly different stories
that added to my knowledge of the war. Sharing past mis-
eries with former combat soldiers brought strength instead
of the intense discomforts caused by talking about the war
with civilians who had only newsprint or TV knowledge.

I had hunted pheasants in South Dakota for years with
midwestern friends. One of these men, Ethan, had served in
the infantry as a machine gunner while in Vietnam. After
a day of hunting late in the evening, Ethan and I would
sometimes sit in the dingy, smoky bar of the Ramkota
Hotel in Pierre, where shadows of mounted deer, elk, and
pheasants peered through the beery air above us.

Ethan hunted as if he were still in a war. He spoke to
six of us while we loaded our shotguns before walking
through a Dakota cornfield, like a squad leader before a
Vietnam patrol. Fingers numb, feet stuck in our icy boots,
we were freezing as he talked.

"All right, men, this is our last day. Only shoot if the

pheasants climb above us. Everyone be careful. Forget shooting at birds flying just above the corn and stubble. Nobody wants to get shot on the last day of hunting."

Ethan's reaction to the sudden takeoff of a pheasant was to empty his gun, to fire three times, and then quickly reload.

After the hunt, we both sat together over a few beers in that Dakota tavern, talking about nothing much except hunting and football and how bad each of us stunk. The conversation often turned to experiences during the Vietnam War. Still wearing his orange vest, Ethan talked first about his experiences.

"I was with a platoon stationed at a fire base near Da Nang. Our captain sent us on a recon because he had been told that the base might soon be attacked by North Vietnamese. We were on patrol from early morning until six at night walking the paddies, going through different hamlets that we knew. There were only a couple of Vietnamese I didn't recognize, but basically, nothing was different.

"About nine o'clock that evening, we were told to double up in the bunkers around the edge of the fire-base hill. About eleven at night, the VC fired rockets. We started to see enemy soldiers coming up the hill. Our Claymore mines had been placed facing downhill—they detected motion and began firing. We also threw hand grenades down the hill. Then the VC started coming in waves. More of our Claymores fired, but the VC just kept coming."

I looked at him. "Couldn't you use the larger guns like the base howitzer?"

"They were too close to use even an M60 machine gun or an M16," Ethan answered, staring at me and holding his weathered hands closer together on our table. I noticed his third and fourth fingers were missing from his left hand.

"Our barbed wire was seven or eight feet high. We were shooting like hell, but some of them got inside the barbwire. Maybe they came in through tunnels, I don't know. They were swarming around us between our bunkers and trying to get into them. I was shooting my .45 pistol at anyone outside of a bunker as I figured none of us was going to be out there. After three or four hours, the fighting died down, and it became quiet with the sunrise. Someone in the next bunker had been shot and killed during the night. Did we do it? Did I do it? How could we have shot him? How could I have shot him?

"An officer said, 'Clean off the razor wires.' So we went out there and pulled the VC bodies off the wires. They were so young. We searched their pockets and found some drugs, some photographs, and a few lucky charms. We pulled them off. Why did they come? I don't know why the hell they kept coming; why the hell would they do that? A few we pulled off the razor wires were still alive.

"One guy said, 'What do we do with them?'

"The sergeant shouted, 'Throw the bastards in the trucks.'

"So we threw them in the trucks. I threw the live ones in the trucks with the dead ones. What were you going to do? I just threw all of them in the trucks. What would happen to them? Buried, burned, hell, I didn't know.

"Helicopters took us back to base camp near the 95th Evacuation Hospital in Da Nang. I was all screwed up and asked to see the hospital priest. He talked with me a day or so later. I told him about the firefight; about the dead GI in the bunker nearest ours; about throwing all the VCs in the trucks whether they were dead or alive.

"The priest said, 'You had to do it, and the Lord is gonna say you had to do it. The Lord is going to forgive you. You've got to put it all behind you.'

"Of course, there is no forgetting what we had done."

We sat there in the darkened bar for a while. The air was close and heavy with smoke and alcohol. Another round of cold, frosty beers appeared. We watched New England beat the crap out of the Bears.

I told Ethan about working with Father Perez the night he helped us remove a soldier from a helicopter who was thought to have a live grenade in his chest. Together, we lifted him out of the helicopter and placed him gently on a stretcher. The soldier looked up at Perez from underneath the pile of sandbags.

"'I know I'm in trouble,' he said.

"'We will hold hands. I will stay with you and pray for you,' Perez told him.

"The hospital CO told us to operate in the morgue. It was separate from the active hospital, and an explosion there would not shut down the treatment of newly wounded arrivals. The room was rapidly cleared of bodies, and the autopsy table surrounded by a circular wall of sandbags to minimize damage to the rest of the hospital if the grenade exploded.

"Perez, along with the doctors, stood beside the soldier lying on the autopsy table inside the ring of sandbags despite the danger of a sudden massive explosion from the rocket-propelled grenade. Not until an X-ray showed only metal fragments left behind by the grenade that must have bounced off the soldier's flak vest did Father move away, using the edge of his vestment to blot his forehead. Later, I found him kneeling on the edge of the helipad, bent over a young child with a fatal brain injury, his hands clasped in prayer beside the weeping mother who cradled her son."

How could we tell these horrors to anyone without similar experiences?

Even though it had been fifty years since Perez and I worked together, I still thought of him often when operating on high-risk patients, especially patients injured in accidents who suffered injuries similar to war wounds. In my mind, I saw him kneeling, holding a patient's hand, offering sacraments, and then looking at me while showing the neck of a tequila bottle in one of his pockets. Just a cap full of that alcohol had seemed so powerful back then. Like a sacrament offering strength and reassurance to face the surgical challenges of treating seriously injured patients.

I never saw or heard more about him after the war until at one of our hospital reunions I was told he had died from cirrhosis of the liver. When important service to others is taken away, by a severe personal injury or by an illness, or

even paradoxically when a war ends, there often is unpro-
ductive time and a sense of loss. I have seen alcohol then
become a seductive solace that becomes an enemy that
eventually destroys a courageous life. I hope after the war,
Father Perez continued helping people in need as he had
done so heroically in Vietnam. That's what I hope.

LIFE IN IOWA (1969–2016)

Several decades passed. Our family lived happily in Iowa.
Mollie was three years old when I returned from Vietnam,
and Susan was born after the war. Only Stephen, then six,
remembered much about the family stresses and worries
during my year in the combat zone.

When they became teenagers, I took each of our children on separate medical missions to Haiti, where they
could see doctors in different specialties donating their
time and working closely together and where research on
tetanus and tuberculosis was underway. I tried to show
them that being a doctor didn't mean you had to be a surgeon or even practice clinical medicine. Somehow they all
became doctors. I take little credit for their career choices.
The high school educational system in Cedar Rapids was
excellent. Many optional courses were available, and the
children were eager to learn. Mimi and my attitudes toward education were similar to our parents'. Homework
came before pleasure, and phone calls after 9:00 p.m. were
strongly discouraged. Stephen became an eye surgeon;
Mollie, an MD, PhD, neuroscientist; and our youngest

child, Susan, a psychiatrist. Perhaps they thought their father needed neurologic or psychiatric help—or at least better eyesight.

RETURN TO EUROPE (OCTOBER 2017)

In 2017, Stephen, now fifty-five years old, asked me to take him to Vietnam so he could learn more about the country and the protracted war and see where I had served as an army surgeon in Da Nang. I had talked with a few veterans who had returned. They were surprised how friendly and helpful the Vietnamese people had been. Even so, I was reluctant to return, not wanting to ignite forgotten horrors. So I suggested to Steve that we travel to Europe and study my father's journey in Patton's army during the Second World War. He liked the idea, so after considerable reading about the war, we carefully planned to follow the course of Patton's Third Army and Dad's 109th Evacuation Hospital during World War II.

Tracing my father's experience brought Steve, Dad, and me closer, even though my dad had died more than two decades before. It was a beautiful October day when my son, Steve, and I arrived in Normandy and stood on Omaha Beach where my father's hospital had come ashore. My dad seemed to be standing beside us. The gently curved sandy beach extended for ten miles with only a few remnants of the crossed iron barriers, once armed with deadly explosives that blocked American tanks and landing craft. Now it looked like a pleasant tourist destination with a few small cafés and walking pathways close to the ocean's edge. A gentle breeze slowly moved flags marking landing sites and pathways farther inland. Small yellow butterflies clustered silently around wildflowers. It was very quiet.

The three of us seemed to be looking at the sites where Dad's hospital had been and at the nearby German trenches and bunkers. Staring at the destroyed tanks and the twisted long-range guns, I almost fell into one of the old German trenches. Steve quickly grabbed my arm and pulled me back from the edge of the ditch. I hadn't been aware that he was looking out for his eighty-four-year-old father. We both smiled. I hadn't thought someday I might need help from our children.

The violence of destruction, of steel against steel, the screams of the wounded could easily be imagined, but instead of causing anxiety or hatred, we were quiet as in a place of worship. I was sad to see all the signs of lost lives. As usual after wars, our hated enemies had become our friends. We were sorry for the losses from either side. Despite almost total destruction of their country, I had several German friends in high school just a few years after the war ended, and the Germans we met in Berlin were friendly and did not try to hide the concentration camps built for eradication of whomever the Nazis had thought inferior. In fact, now the Germans insisted that their schoolchildren visit those preserved camps and see the photographs showing Nazis torturing and killing their "inferiors." We stood side by side in sorrowful silence with people from Germany, staring at unbelievable acts of cruelty.

After following the course of Patton's Third Army across Europe, I realized visiting these battle sites had increased my knowledge of the war but had not brought back old, unwanted dreams of worry about my father when I was a youngster. It wasn't closure; I had never believed in closure. But learning more about the war and learning where Dad had been in the Battle of the Bulge when his hospital was captured eased my mind. The patients and the medical staff were evacuated safely just before the hospital was lost, and he returned uninjured after the war. He never talked about the details of the fighting, but perhaps just kept taking care of all the wounded and would have continued to do so even if he had been captured.

The flood of German pistols, the Mauser rifle and bloodied German flag, the gas masks, and swastika daggers told us enough. He escaped. That was enough. It was what we had prayed for. Steve and I shared the scenes of battle and, together, saw the sacrifices from both sides. At Bastogne, we shared a large table with a German family before visiting the museum and surrounding countryside. We shared our food and drank beers as a toast to each other's health. Friendships with former enemies, a restoration of faith in humanity, were helpful in forgetting the long-ago worries and uncertainties.

That trip to Europe changed my mind about returning to Vietnam. Wouldn't more knowledge about the war and learning what had happened to the people of South Vietnam after the war be helpful for Steve, our family, and for me? I had heard from veterans who had returned to that country that war damages had mostly been repaired and many new buildings constructed. And more surprising to me, they all mentioned that the Vietnamese loved Americans. I wondered if any Vietnamese doctors I had worked with during the war were still alive. What was left of the American Evacuation Hospital?

I thought about the heat and humidity. Except for the monsoon season, I had been soaked with sweat for months. Older now, I had much less tolerance for the heat than during the war years and less energy. I doubt I would have undertaken the journey without Steve.

RETURN TO VIETNAM (JANUARY 2020)

It was fifty years after I'd last been there, but sitting on the plane with my son, I remembered the dread when we landed in Da Nang in 1968 after flying from California and refueling in Honolulu and Guam. We were halfway around the world from home and in a war zone. Back then we stood beside soldiers waiting to return home after a year in the combat zone. They called us "fucking new guys" and shouted warnings to us: "Keep your fucking head down; keep your M16 clean, and shoot anything that moves."

In 1968, we had flown in darkness most of the way and approached the city from the east over the ocean in a steep, spiraled dive. The unusual approach was to avoid enemy gunfire. Welcome to Vietnam. We taxied to a military hangar; the airplane door opened, and hot, humid air burst into the 707, its aluminum skin still cold to my touch. We lined up and walked to the barracks with our duffel bags. The outside thermometer read 104 degrees.

A pudgy, sweating, sunburned sergeant had welcomed us in 1968 with the remark that we would have experiences over the next year to tell our grandchildren. "Interesting experiences," he said. I just wanted to eventually *have* grandchildren.

***

Now, fifty years later, I returned to Vietnam with our son. We approached Vietnam again over the South China Sea, but the descent was shallow, smooth, and comfortable. After landing, Steve and I walked along the air-conditioned skyway, passed quickly through customs and immigration lines, and met our guide just outside the airport entrance. Mr. Thong stood beside a small Toyota, holding a cardboard sign printed neatly: "MEFFERT." It was hot and humid like it had been fifty years ago. But the smells of rotting fish and market refuse had been replaced by exhaust fumes from hundreds of screaming motorbikes roaring over smooth asphalt. The city, even at first view, was unrecognizable to me. No military vehicles, guns, or khaki-dressed soldiers. Many high-rise condos, apartments, and resorts lined the beachfronts; recently built, pristine, air-conditioned, and sparsely occupied. In the car, I asked our guide, Thong, where the money for the reconstruction had come from.

Thong looked back at us from his front seat and rubbed

his fingers like he was sorting dollar bills. "Chinese," he added, then turned to look at the crowded traffic through the windshield. The pristine buildings, the smooth asphalt roads, and modern airport had replaced the odor of burning charcoal, the rusted, corrugated shacks, the open-air food markets, and all the dirt roads crowded by farm animals. Now Da Nang was a modern beachfront resort city, but tourists were scarce. New bridges, one with a golden, crouching dragon extending over the water, spanned the dark Han River, which flowed slowly like syrup into the ocean. Thong pointed out a new high-rise hospital as we arrived at our hotel, which was part of a beachfront compound.

"Where are the people who lived outdoors, the people who wore rags, those without homes who lived on the streets? Is there a problem with drug addiction?" I asked him.

Thong turned again to answer. "The sick people are put in hospitals; we shoot the drug dealers."

Steve looked over at me, his eyes widened. "Bullshit," I think he said.

I remembered, during the war, the destitute tin-roofed, palm-branched shacks that crowded our hospital, the fishermen, and their families waiting for treatment of parasitic illnesses, malaria, and for surgery. They were also visited at night by VC. We couldn't provide complete security. They had played both sides. Isn't that what we would have done? Isn't that what desperate people do in any war? They try to protect themselves any way that seems less risky.

But what did the VC do to all these people after the war? We passed large cemeteries without a comment from Thong. We didn't think he wanted to talk about what had happened to people living in small villages, the fishermen, the beggars, or the wandering ill who had clustered around our hospital, dressed in rags and subsisting on fish and a few vegetables. When they had been injured or wounded, we took care of them, often finding clusters of worms crowding their intestines. They could not have all moved away from their shacks without a relocation program.

It was hard to imagine that this move could have been voluntary. Both Stephen and I thought they must have been moved by the government or even eliminated. They had just disappeared, and nobody would talk about how that had happened.

The beach had been transformed into a series of hotels and condominiums, and tourists were welcome. We both asked who had built these resorts and again where the poor and ill people had been placed, where they had been taken. Thong looked at us and rubbed his hands, indicating an exchange of money. As far as Stephen and I knew, only the Chinese had that amount of money. The young Vietnamese working in these new buildings spoke excellent English and were exceedingly courteous.

The city was so different. The old and the new felt disconnected.

"Dad, don't you wonder what really happened to all those people in rags living along the streets and the crowds of people pulling carts of vegetables and carrying clusters of bound chickens in your photos? Were they killed? Relocated by force? How could they otherwise all disappear?"

But the old memories of insecurity, wounded soldiers, and close calls did not return, not until Steve and I took a late-afternoon walk along the sandy beach at the ocean's edge. Then darkness came suddenly like years before. Like blowing out a match. The horizon faded to a blurred haze. Light, all light, was replaced by a heavy, thick darkness, a blackness palpable as stone. Just like before, my head felt separated from my hands, and smashing waves erased other sounds. Disoriented, I didn't know which way to walk or even which way to turn. I remembered why at night, years ago, I had rarely walked in darkness along the beach outside the hospital compound. *Charley* might have been right beside me. The evacuation hospital reappeared in my mind. Memories of helicopters, heavy gunfire, and streams of wounded flooded back. I stood still and listened carefully.

A thought recurred from the war years that my family was literally on the opposite side of the world. I was as far away on Earth as possible from them. Again, I had trouble seeing their images; just some conversations remained. Music was playing behind me where several lights pointed away from the water's edge. Steve must have noticed my hesitation and silence.

"Dad, let's have a drink at the bar and listen to the music. Can't see a thing out here, and the waves make too much noise." We turned from the ocean and walked over the loose sand back to our hotel.

A few days before we arrived, our guide, Thong, mentioned to a neighbor he was going to show two American doctors around Da Nang. Surprisingly, his neighbor said he knew a Vietnamese neurosurgeon who had worked with an American surgeon at the 95th Evacuation Hospital, where I was assigned during the war. The following day, over a midmorning tea, Thong introduced Steve and me to Dr. Dung. He had decided to stay in South Vietnam when it was lost to the North Vietnamese over fifty years ago. He had a large family and not enough money to try for an escape, but his brothers were able to leave the country and came to America. Thong told us that Dr. Dung and his family were sent to a camp after the war, where he was "reeducated" for two years before being released and permitted to enter a surgical practice that barely provided for his family. Dr. Dung had known Dr. Phouc, the Vietnamese surgeon I had often worked with years ago. They had trained in the same French medical school. He knew that Dr. Phouc had died five years ago from a heart attack. But he also knew Phouc had two sons in the United States.

Sitting in the living room of his home, I stared at Dr. Dung. He looked familiar. Had we met during the war? His face had just a few wrinkles. His hair was black, the same as it must have been fifty years ago. Dr. Dung mentioned he had worked with a neurosurgeon from our army hospital. Then I remembered an old photo of Dr. Phouc and three other Vietnamese doctors taken one late afternoon after finishing surgery years ago. Despite his capture, and a deprived life during the two years of forced education and a supervised medical practice, he looked healthy and spoke excellent English. I told him he had aged well, better than I had. He looked at my bald head. His hairline was unchanged from fifty years ago. We laughed after he told me he dyed his hair, mentioning it was a common thing for Vietnamese men to do as they aged. He looked considerably younger than his age of eighty-four and was recognizable from that old photograph taken outside the civilian hospital and still in my files at home. Despite his age, he was seeing patients some afternoons in an old garage converted to a medical office beside his home.

"I have to. We had so damn many children," he said, and we both laughed.

We talked about other MDs, both Vietnamese and American, that we had known. All were now incapacitated or had died. The sunlight was fading when we left his home with our guide and Dr. Dung to take a short drive toward Monkey Mountain along the smooth asphalt road to find exactly where the 95th American Evacuation Hospital had been. There was no trace of the Quonset Huts or any hospital equipment. Even the large helipad had disappeared beneath a smooth four-lane highway with the ocean and beach sand on one side and a string of run-down shops on the other. Instead of helicopters and the odor of kerosene, now automobiles roared past us on that highway beside a wide brick walkway, bright restaurant umbrellas, and spicy odors of Asian food.

Nothing remained of the hospital despite the thousands

of civilians and soldiers from both sides treated there and the hundreds of people saved from death by its emergency services. It seemed wrong, even unconscionable, that the hospital would not even be acknowledged. Not even a sign on a post to indicate where it had been. Instead, there was this wide, asphalt boulevard. Dung and I shared tears and even some laughs. Neither one of us had ever spoken much about our wartime experiences, but now previously forgotten memories of operating on soldiers and civilians just poured out.

Standing there, I recalled the look on Dr. Phouc's face fifty years ago when I had asked him to insert his index finger into the left atrium of a woman's heart and feel her mitral valve narrowed to a pencil-sized opening by rheumatic fever. And his wide-eyed look replaced by a smile when he felt the valve after it had been opened to a normal size.

He and I had repaired freaks of trauma together: I remembered one patient drank orange Kool-Aid and then laughed as crowds of patients at the civilian hospital shouted and pointed when, after several seconds, the liquid came out of a hole in his chest. Another had an aneurysm of a subclavian artery from a gunshot injury to his chest wall. The damaged artery was extremely thin-walled; blood could be seen swirling just under the patient's skin. Urgently, we transferred the patient to the American Evacuation Hospital for vascular surgery and removed the aneurysm that same night, using a plastic artery to supply blood to his arm. I often wondered how many civilians had died because the bullet or shrapnel had caused an injury slightly different, just a few millimeters closer to vital anatomic structures.

Once Dr. Phouc and I were removing a tuberculous lung from a young woman at the civilian hospital. The patient's breathing tube fell out of her windpipe. The blood turned dark. It had fallen out twice before during the operation. Phouc stepped up to the patient's head, pushed the anesthetist aside, and replaced the breathing tube into the trachea. There was a short, loud exchange in Vietnamese. "What did you say?" I asked him. With a straight face, Dr. Phouc said, "Use more goddamn fucking tape."

We had operated on so many odd cases together during the war. Hundreds of them were civilians. Standing on the army hospital site with Steve, Dr. Dung told us about cases of head trauma he and an American neurosurgeon had cared for. I recalled helping that same surgeon fashion a replacement for part of a soldier's missing skull with plastic resin; after activation it became very warm as it hardened to protect the soldier's brain.

We talked for another hour or longer later in the afternoon, standing alongside the four-lane boulevard. I promised to send him the old photograph I had of him at home. We shook hands and embraced. There were more tears. I had no memory of crying like this. Then I felt Steve's arm around me and was greatly comforted. It was time to leave. I thought about how it was very unlikely we would ever meet Dr. Dung again.

***

The following day, we travelled from Da Nang to Quang
Tri and the former marine base of Khe Sanh in the northern part of South Vietnam. The driver of our car was Tin,
a rubbery, uncreased teenager who remained almost cata-
tonic whether kilometers or millimeters separated us from
other traffic while we drove north to Khe Sanh and the
former demilitarized zone. Thong, our guide, as usual, sat
in front beside our driver. After looking at how near the
rapidly closing motor scooters came, he turned to talk to
us in the back seat about events happening during the previous century that he thought had led to the Vietnam War.
Thong might have looked away from the rushing traffic
more often, but like a retired soldier, still had a stiff neck
from before.

During the long drive, I thought about all the fighting
that had taken place north of Da Nang fifty years ago in
Quang Tri Province, the city of Quang Tri, Khe Sanh, and
along the DMZ. Our evacuation hospital had admitted
many soldiers who had been wounded there. The fighting
had been almost constant north of Da Nang, and the flow
of wounded from that part of the country had been steady
the entire year I worked as a combat surgeon. After initial treatment at smaller hospitals, many of the seriously
wounded casualties had been flown in helicopters to our
hospital in Da Nang. One of our duties was to make certain that wounded American soldiers had been correctly
diagnosed and treated before evacuation from the country.

Sometimes additional surgery was required before the soldiers were stable or additional problems were discovered needing treatment before sending them home.

I was curious to see how the enemy was able to provide large numbers of soldiers and weapons across the demilitarized zone. That infiltration probably would have been more difficult without the rules of combat forbidding our army from advancing into North Vietnam. But if the war had been extended, would China have entered the war with its millions of soldiers? Would that extension have eventually triggered a nuclear war? Steve and I talked about this and the often-unforeseen events that happen later in a war not anticipated at its beginning.

Steve looked over at me. "If the Chinese had entered the war, we might have used nuclear weapons. Their response might have been nuclear also. You might have never come home, Dad."

When in Da Nang fifty years ago, I had thought the same thing.

"Or what if there had been a wise settlement of the Indochina territorial dispute after World War Two?" I added.

The roads from Da Nang north to the city of Quang Tri and farther southwest to Khe Sanh were now smoothly paved with asphalt instead of gravel. Motorbike repair shops, gasoline stations, and shops filled with old clothing cloistered the road's edge. Gusty winds blew clouds of dust across the road while hundreds of motorbikes roared beside us along Highways 1 and 9. It was hot and humid.

After an hour of driving, Thong pointed out a small stony mountain to our right called the Rockpile; its huge, irregular boulders and sheer cliffs had provided a natural defense for American reconnaissance.

Thong looked back at us again. "Did you know that no marines on that mountain were ever killed in combat?" he said. "Getting orders for the Rockpile was almost a guarantee of survival. It was impossible for the North Vietnamese to approach and climb it with their weapons without being seen."

Remembering all the wounded soldiers we had treated from fighting near that mountain, what Thong said seemed unlikely.

We visited several American Special Forces camps that had supported the defense of Khe Sanh during the siege starting in 1968. The camps were primitive first defenses around Khe Sanh. Just sandbags, guns, radios, and a few heavily built shelters. Several of these had been overrun during the siege. I had treated a few severely wounded American marines who had survived in these camps and had fought their way back to Khe Sanh.

Thong said that American forces held Khe Sanh during seventy-eight days of heavy shelling by NVA troops firing long-range artillery shells from surrounding mountains. The marine base was in a flat valley surrounded by mountains—a difficult place to hold against the enemies who looked down with their howitzers and long-range guns.

I looked at the surrounding hills and mountains. They seemed far away from the marine base. How could they accurately target each other? I imagined the NVA could look down and see where their shells hit the base and make corrections visually. I'm certain they must have had more-accurate aiming techniques. The American marines must also have had ways of tracking the big guns of the enemy in the surrounding mountains. B-52 bombers pulverized the mountains with heavy bombs, and smaller jets hit targets with napalm on the flat plain closer to the base. Five hundred Americans were killed. Fifteen thousand NVA lost their lives. Those numbers seemed impossible as I scanned across Khe Sanh's flat, quiet valley and the green, peaceful-looking mountains.

We pulled into a small gravel parking lot beside Khe Sanh. Steve and I got out of the car. Nothing much of the base remained. It was hot, dry, and looked deserted. An old man dressed in a ragged North Vietnamese uniform walked the sparse grass around the small Khe Sanh museum. He tried to sell old, worn-out Vietnamese uniforms and faded North Vietnamese Army badges. Several Vietnamese sat in a tin shack, selling bottled water, homemade purses, jewelry made from bullets, and shell fragments that had been gathered from the ground near the broken, eroded runway. A few corroded American aircraft and helicopters littered the valley. Several worn-out howitzers and rusted tanks were scattered haphazardly in the surrounding weeds. Just a few buildings remained; they were mostly underground with narrow slit windows, reinforced walls, and sandbagged roofs. Deep zigzagged trenches linked the buildings, constructed to minimize the effect of artillery shells striking the pathways. Walking or even running from one building to another had invited instant NVA gunfire.

The sandbags and trenches must have offered some protection from enemy bombardments, but I couldn't imagine living for months with daily and nightly artillery fire and crawling like a mole through the trenches to the buildings. The unending noise of artillery, the sniper fire, the probing attacks from both sides—it must have been terrifying. Running on the ground from building to building above the revetments would have been like playing Russian roulette with enemy sniper fire. The marines had been under constant, unpredictable shellfire for seventy-eight days.

Now the only sound was a raw northern wind blowing brown dust over remnants that looked more like a staged movie set than a former battleground. We were the only visitors I could see. We walked a few trenches, bent over as marines must have run them. We looked into several buildings dug into the ground; just narrow windows and sandbags visible from the outside. Nothing remained inside them except dirt floors and bare dirt walls with a few rusted nails that perhaps had been used to hang weapons and uniforms. I thought of the thousands of soldiers killed, wounded, or psychologically maimed from both sides. Khe Sanh had been the prize. But was it really? Perhaps the entire fight had been a sham by the North Vietnamese to draw attention to the besieged marine base and to cause American soldiers who normally protected Hue, Quang Tri, and Da Nang to be sent to Khe Sanh before the large urban battles erupted during Tet. Now the abandoned marine base should be a monument of hope for settling arguments peacefully rather than with war. Instead, there were just an old, demented Vietnamese man selling rusted medals, a few others selling trinkets and bottled water, and Thong, Steve, and me. Everyone else had left. We stood there beside rusted war relics. The three of us were quiet, looking down at the dusty brown earth and the distant, faded mountains. I was quite depressed. Compared with Khe Sanh, we had been somewhat secure in Da Nang, even while treating hundreds of terrible, unforgettable wounds of war.

I walked out of the museum while a propaganda movie was showing. Steve watched the film while loudspeakers played marches and a jerky, yellowed video showed a US plane shot down in flames. In the video, Jane Fonda sat smiling beside a North Vietnamese antiaircraft gun.

***

While I waited, I thought about how the generals and politicians had wanted to draw the enemy together, to group the NVA armies for a sustained, constricting attack of Khe Sanh similar to the encirclement of Dien Bien Phu years before. But massive B-52 bombing and the use of napalm caused thousands of casualties, and the NVA finally withdrew. After the battle, Khe Sanh was abandoned by our marines. To them, the battle had been a success in terms of body counts. It seemed a bizarre way to conduct a war.

How can you kill more of the enemy than your own troop loses, then abandon the base and call the whole episode a victory? What was the going price for those bodies? It was just a larger version of the fight over a hill near our hospital in Da Nang. That hill was captured and then given up three times by our marines during the year I was in Da Nang. Twenty or thirty marines were lost with each attack; each time, slippery blood covered our hospital floors, and piles of M16 rifles, helmets, flak vests, and cutaway, blood-soaked American uniforms crowded against the walls of the admissions ward. But the kill ratio was in favor of our side, so each time the fighting was called a victory no matter what Hanoi Hannah said. All those arms and legs, the bodies and deranged body parts—all the dead and wounded just for a small, rocky hill? And each time we had given the hill back. If only the generals could have given back all those soldiers.

***

As I was waiting for Steve on the wooden steps of the museum, a young North Vietnamese soldier sat down next to me. Dressed in a carefully pressed NVA uniform without wrinkles despite the heat, he spoke excellent English. I showed him a few old photographs of our Da Nang military hospital that I had downloaded on my phone. We took photos of each other. No stranger to modern conveniences, he pulled out his own cell phone to share his photographs with a few flicks of his thumbs. His grandfather had been a North Vietnamese soldier who was killed in the battle, probably from a B-52 bombardment. This young man was now in charge of the museum with rusted, corroded rifles, wide-mouthed mortars, and two worn-out howitzers scattered across the floors. On one of the walls, Jane Fonda smiled, and waves of North Vietnamese soldiers charged forward with fixed bayonets. We talked about soldiers from both sides killed in the battle. His grandfather was one of the thousands killed trying to capture the marine base. Only a few photographs remained of his grandfather. I told the young NVA soldier about operating on many GIs wounded in fighting north of Da Nang and that I was very sorry about his grandfather's death. How much both sides had lost. We shared tears and agreed that for either side, the war had not been worth the sacrifices. Then he stood and walked slowly back to the museum while I stayed sitting there, thinking about how the suffering from this war, like all wars, had been much greater than just the lost soldiers. The people killed from each side had been connected to families. They lost the sharing of family love and the advice, the guidance for children and grandchildren that might have been given. Their entire future was lost, and thousands of families were irreparably torn apart.

I remembered the many times my father had taken our three children on nature walks on his farm. He had been a gentle, loving teacher. His grandchildren had learned to carefully study prairie flowers and birds, and how to discover four-leaf clovers even in a crowded pasture. They

explored the small creek on his farm, where fish and turtles lived. Dad created quiet and careful ways for them to
learn and instilled toughness by taking them on long, hot
journeys through wide native pastures. All three children
became interested in science and became physicians.

***

It was hot and very humid, so I remained sitting on the
steps of the museum in the shade of a few spindly trees
while waiting for Steve, and thought about how my father had influenced our lives and how fortunate we were
that he had survived the war in Europe. This young North
Vietnamese soldier hadn't known his grandfather. There
had been no nature walks, and no shared love. When the
grandfather was killed, part of this young soldier was also
lost.

Steve finally showed up. He had left the Khe Sanh
museum and walked through several tunnels dug during
the war by the North Vietnamese Army to pass their soldiers unobserved across the demilitarized zone into South
Vietnam. He knew I wouldn't want to do that. He said it
was too hot, and he had to wade through standing water in
some of the tunnels, and the lighting was very poor. Then
he looked down at me.

"Dad, I'm glad you weren't with me. I know your worst
fear is being buried alive."

I don't remember ever telling him that, but somehow

he knew. I thanked him for his good judgment. We sat for a while longer in that small patch of shade. He brought up more memories of my father.

"I thought of Grandpa as a wise and clever teacher of nature and practical things," Steve said. "As a child myself, I enjoyed his almost childlike curiosity about the world around him and his interest in learning even the little things. He would show me in minute detail how to cook steak on his tiny charcoal grill on his back step. Today, his teaching still causes me to think about perfecting techniques of simple tasks and even surgery."

I pulled out my iPhone and pressed the record button. This seemed important.

"I remember catching a snapping turtle when I was twelve. Grandpa said if I could carry it back to the farmhouse, he'd show me how to kill and clean it and we'd have it for lunch. I had to hold the twelve-pound snapping turtle by its slippery tail and away from me to avoid being bitten. On the way back to his house, we met Donny, his closest neighbor, who was disking weeds on his tractor in a nearby cornfield. They talked and talked while I held the turtle by its tail, feeling like my arm was about to fall off."

"I'm glad he was at least a little hard on you," I said. "I remember his criticisms and dares more than the compliments or gentle teaching. Maybe he was always tired. He was on duty every night and weekend unless he took vacations. The phone in our hallway rang frequently at night. He would answer a 'yello,' then pause while listening as a new problem was explained. There were often out-of-town emergencies. That's what I really liked."

He would sometimes take me with him at night, even into operating rooms, especially on the weekends. I would stand at the doorway of a patient's room while Dad explained to the patient and family what he thought the problem was and what needed to be done. I didn't understand a lot about what had happened or what needed to be repaired, but he used simple words that even I could understand to explain problems to the family. He was kind and more patient in teaching about things that went wrong in the human body than when he showed me how to fix things around the house.

I thought about trying to explain why Dad's behavior was sometimes not predictable, but Steve had not experienced that. He thought Dad was an interesting, loving teacher. And I couldn't deny he was that. I decided not to talk about how I thought Dad had sometimes been unreasonably short-tempered and demanding with me when I was a youngster. I thought again about what Dad used to tell me when I had a problem. He would stand there, a hand holding his chin, and look at the situation. "There has to be a solution. You just haven't thought of it yet."

It is still engraved deeply somewhere in my brain and passed on to our children's brains. Many things he told me had been acts of love, spoken briefly and without emotion; similar to his talking to patients and their families about serious medical problems. He spoke to them as if he were a family member, and they seemed to understand. And hadn't it been an act of love to take me with him during those night emergencies? It must have been awkward for him to drag this young kid along, to pin scrubs on my small body, and to tell me where to stand and what to do if I felt strange or dizzy.

***

The following day, Steve and I flew from Hue to Saigon. I wouldn't have recognized this city. Hazy, choked with smog, with numerous high-rise buildings and crowds pressing together in the city of thirteen million people. I had only been in downtown once during the war. At that time, the once-graceful but then war-neglected mansions extended along the Saigon River. They were reminders of the French control of the country before World War II. Fifty years ago, the downtown was filled with outdoor food markets selling slabs of raw meat, live animals hanging from iron rafters over sidewalks, and crowds of people buying black-market American Cokes, beer, candy, and T-shirts. The smell of burning charcoal, the delicate perfume of well-shaped bar girls in sleazy honky-tonks, blaring Western pop, flocks of bicycles and three-wheeled pedicabs. I remembered the disorienting cacophony. But now, modern factories, many stores, hotels, and a large international airport had changed everything. The Vietnamese were friendly and helpful.

Our guide, about twenty-five years old, spoke excellent English. His name was Juan. Our new driver was older, almost sedate, and nicknamed Hero for good reason. In Saigon, motorbikes made Hue's traffic seem like kindergarten. There was literally no space between cars and bikes. Aggressive motorbike riders cooperated in opening pathways through heavy traffic so streams of motorbikes could follow behind, shutting off cars and bikes going in slightly different directions.

If we had tried, it would have been possible to reach out of our car window and steer the nearest motorbike while the rider used both hands to light a cigarette. And yet I never saw a street accident. Misses were by millimeters. Sometimes it felt like our car was suspended off the roadway by motorbikes and carried like a stick floating rapidly down a river. Our driver seemed unconcerned; he often yawned—after all, he was a "Hero."

***

The temperature in Saigon was in the high nineties with humidity over 80 percent, perhaps even hotter in the Mekong Delta area of southern Vietnam, the final area of the country we planned to visit. I had heard soldiers talk about the vast maze of the delta rivers, the unending swamps and small islands, the mud of the rice paddies, and the jungle encroachment of waterways, making ambushes of patrol boats easy for the VC. Our army had responded with Agent Orange to kill the dense vegetation of the riverbanks, but many places remained near the rivers and streams for the VC to hide, including tunnels, narrow water tributaries concealed with brush, and the remaining nearby jungle. Illnesses, including dengue fever, malaria, and rodent-borne diseases, were common in that part of the country during the war.

I was hoping to visit the delta with Steve because I had never been there and had only read about the fighting along rivers and the narrow-waterway ambushes, but I hadn't slept well for the past two nights and had lost my energy. I decided to remain in our hotel. The thought of the delta day trip, the hiking, the biking along jungle trails, and travelling in a sampan to a lunch in a boiling, humid jungle just didn't suit me. It was very humid, and the temperature was forecast to be in the high nineties. But Steve was eager to see the delta and travel there with our guide, Juan.

I remained in our hotel room with gloomy thoughts, not able to rid the despair of war. I remembered the soldiers wounded and the soldiers no longer alive, as if fifty years ago were just earlier in the day. We all carry earlier times in our minds, bidden or unbidden, the good with the bad. These memories crowd others at times, and then they in turn become crowded. It happens without direction. It happens like aging. Alone in the hotel room during the day, I wrote about Khe Sanh. Then, after a break for lunch, I wrote about little things, interesting little things we had seen during our first day in Saigon:

The motorbikes roaring noisily along in clouds of oily exhaust, often ridden by goggled, delicate women, cutting aggressively into traffic as if a place had been reserved for them, their *ao dais* streaming behind them. Their expressions unreadably calm while rushing past us in the gray pollution, the heat, and the obvious danger of collisions.

"They are beautiful," I had said to Juan.

"Yes, yes," he answered, laughing. "My wife sees them too. She says she will cut off my cucumber if I fool around."

I had ordered hot tea for dinner last night. Our waitress was pretty and pleasant.

Smiling, she said, "Oh, we don't have hot tea."

"Well then, I'll have a hot Coke," I replied. Then her delicate young laugh.

The following morning, the sun shone onto my hands through one of our room windows. I looked down at my fingers.

Once they had been straight, eager, powerful, and well skinned. Now they were bent, arthritic, brown-spotted, and thinly wrinkled. Yet well educated. They had learned a lot from the many years, and so had I.

It was cool and quiet in our hotel room. I searched my thoughts about relations with other people, how fragile they can be and how easily they may change. I remembered the photos of World War II enemies shown on the screen in downtown movie theaters. There was a countdown after Germany and Italy surrendered. "Two Down, One to Go" was the headline. Only Tojo remained.

I hadn't thought much about the Vietnam War during my residency after volunteering to enter the army following six years of surgical training. I thought by then the war would be over. Perhaps I still harbored negative views of

Asians from World War II. But orders for Vietnam arrived. I was frightened but rapidly reeducated in Da Nang while working with many Vietnamese surgeons. They were eager to learn how American doctors treated major trauma. Some I worked with had not finished surgical training; they had been drafted and exposed to major trauma without previously learning how to manage many difficult surgical problems such as how to control major intra-abdominal hemorrhage, how to repair major liver injuries, or even injuries to the abdominal vena cava. They had worked hard and were eager to learn. Then, when we left South Vietnam, many, like Dr. Dung, were sent to reeducation camps, and probably many more were killed. Now I mourn their loss, including that of Dr. Phouc and his family.

A few years after World War II, my father drove a Volkswagen, and I had close German friends in high school. Two years ago, the Germans had been friendly when Steve and I visited Berlin. Now here we were in Vietnam, crying with the grandsons of men we had once tried to kill. I thought about that young NVA soldier I met at Khe Sanh just a few days earlier. Hatred during the war had been fed by fear and propaganda. For both of us, that hatred had been replaced by sorrow for the dead and wounded and for what we both had lost. We had parted with sympathy; I was truly sorry for the loss of his grandfather. Hate is infectious; love is delicate and easily damaged, but more persistent, as is compassion. Evil eventually loses, and in my experience, enemies usually become friends.

***

Steve returned to the hotel late in the afternoon, soiled and sweaty. After he showered, we sat in our room, enjoying its cool air while he described the delta fighting he'd learned about from his guide. "The fighting had been along muddy trails and in muddy water," he said, as if I didn't remember myself stories about the soaked rice fields, the hidden ambushes and sudden firefights along overgrown trails and the small, hidden waterways. I listened uncomfortably, my mind filling with visions of the wounded soldiers I'd seen.

Later, in the evening, we walked down a spiral staircase from our room to the hotel lounge. A young Vietnamese woman stood near the lounge windows, one hand touching a piano, the other holding a small microphone. She sang quietly, and the piano played softly while her white *ao dai* swayed gently to a rhythm unknown to me. We sat in one of the softly padded sofas and talked quietly about our family and what the years had brought. I asked him if he remembered when I was in Vietnam.

"I don't remember much from that age, except you called home one night from Texas to tell us about your Vietnam orders. Mom hardly ever cried, but she cried that night. I was a worried nine-year-old. Mom told me years later that when she told me the news, I had reached up, wrapped my arms around her waist, and told her we would just pretend that Dad was at the hospital and would be home soon."

There was a pause while a waitress brought us drinks.

"Did you raise your children differently than you were raised?"

He and Melissa have two children, now in their twenties. Their older daughter, Liana, is in medical school. She somehow finds time to write meaningful poetry that has been widely published. She has found her passion. Clarice is younger with evolving thoughts about her career and continued necessary education. Both are very intelligent and quite independent. I thought they had been raised with fewer rules than our children. Then Steve replied, "Well, Dad, I'm probably more relaxed about most things than you are. And it was a different time when we raised our children; a less authoritarian time, with fewer family rules and more self-direction."

"And no war," I added.

"Sometimes it seemed to Mimi and me that you were headed for serious trouble while still in high school," I said. "Weekends were difficult for a few years. You often got home long after we asked you to; we worried until hearing your old Ford come up the driveway. I drove it once for some reason. There was a rattling in the trunk. I stopped, opened the trunk, and found dozens of empty beer cans.

"Remember the fights we had, the disagreements even when you were in college?"

"And you sold my car. I was furious. But you and Mom were fair and evenhanded with each of us. You didn't choose favorites and told us that each of us could accomplish whatever we wanted if we put our minds to it.

"Mom told me I had to have a job if I returned home after my first year in college. I came home as usual, but without a summer job. Less than a week later, Mom called the owner of a Wyoming ranch where we had once vacationed and offered me as a laborer for the summer. Mostly I dug ditches with another guy who was recovering from some addiction. That was a turning point for me."

I thought that Mimi had been very brave to set up that ranch job. I could picture Steve riding shirtless on horseback or driving a beat-up ranch pickup truck filled with spades and spare irrigation parts, stopping to shoot groundhogs with his rifle. His summer days in Wyoming provided an up-close view of an alternative life. They were long and hot, and always exhausting. It was much different from the mountain vacations our family had taken when he was younger.

And Mimi had done it herself. She showed me the bus tickets just several days before Steve left home.

"Never bet against your mother," I said. "She thinks carefully, knows many people, and makes good decisions, often on her own. I wasn't home much in the army and when beginning my surgical practice. As my dad said when he left for Europe, 'Take care of the family.' That's what she's always done."

"Dad, you were more direct," Steve said. "Looking back, I guess I wasn't surprised at your hard-ass attitude. It takes a certain type of person to be confident enough to think it's acceptable and desirable that they alone should be allowed to cut into another person's body. A part of the package of personality traits not necessarily endearing, but useful in a surgical environment."

I laughed. Steve had graduated high in his medical class and is widely known as a meticulous, precise retinal surgeon with excellent judgment. For years, he has assisted new surgeons joining the practice until certain of their technical ability. Yet he appears calm and relaxed.

"You keep those hard-ass traits more hidden than I. Perhaps it's your mother's influence."

I wasn't tracking the time. We'd had several gin and tonics. Just a few guests remained in the lounge, and the Vietnamese woman still sang quietly with words I had long forgotten. I looked at the dark night through large glass windows behind the piano. A blue neon Caravelle Hotel sign glowed high from a nearby building. I remembered many western correspondents had stayed there during the war. I'd heard about the blaring American music and the rooftop garden laughter. It had been a safe place to hear stories. Some of their reports might have been gathered in bars and hotels rather than from actual battles.

Now there was a soft calmness in our hotel. We still sat comfortably listening to the singing and the piano. I couldn't remember spending any other time with Steve that was as uninterrupted and quiet.

"I feel old," I said.

"You are, Dad. But young for your age." We smiled. It wasn't a joke. I thought about aging. My own. My dad's. My son's.

I was comfortable that night thinking about aging. Who is the person they were fifty years ago? I remembered when Steve became stronger than I was; I could not loosen his grip on my arm when we wrestled one night, and I recalled my teenage years, when I had thrown my dad down during a long-ago wrestling match one summer. And that day decades ago when I'd operated on Dad's damaged heart. Who had been stronger that day? These rites of passage no longer bothered me.

One evening after dinner, Steve and I were walking down a flight of thickly carpeted stairs in our Saigon hotel. I caught my foot for a second. He reached out and grasped my arm. I wouldn't have fallen without his help. But it was still comforting to feel his grip, to know he was there, and to realize that our love for each other was just as strong, even though different now than it had been before. He had become my caretaker without being asked, and I didn't mind. I was surprised, though, at his sudden move. He had also been watchful when we talked with Dr. Dung a few days before. I looked at those photographs someone had taken of us. We stood there, Steve, Dr. Dung, and I. We had been talking about my good friend Dr. Phouc, the surgeon I had often operated with during the war. He had assisted me while operating on patients in heart failure from damaged mitral valves. He had been so encouraging in finding and preparing those young adults for surgery. They would have died without his hard work of preparation. Now he had also died. His heart had worn out. I looked again at that photograph of Steve standing beside me and

Dr. Dung. Steve's arm was across my back, his hand on my other shoulder. I hadn't felt it.

It seemed my father was sitting nearby on the lounge sofa. Sipping Scotch, he laughed softly.

"Not the surgeon you used to be, but you still have a lot to give others."

I looked at him in my mind; shorter now, kinder than I remembered, honest, still driven, and still tough.

I never saw him give up, not even when playing golf. We searched the weeds for his damn ball until he found a ball, *his* ball, while other golfers played past us. I had watched him operate many times, but had never seen him give up hope of saving someone with a complicated surgical problem. It had been attitude training for me, whether I then realized it or not.

There has to be a solution. You just haven't thought of it yet.

He said that when we talked about problems.

"Let's both try to be more kind." I imagined turning and saying that to him, his ghost version, sitting beside us in that Saigon hotel later in the evening.

ACKNOWLEDGMENTS

Thank you, readers, for taking time to stand closely to the people of this book.

To all Vietnam combat soldiers, and their families.

To victims of all wars. May those responsible see what they have done.

To Hans Steiner, Randy Weingarten, Audrey Shafer, Irvin Yalom, and other Pegasus Physician Writers at Stanford who consistently urged me to look deeper.

To my family and friends who toiled through the revisions of this story and offered valuable comments.

To Laurel Braitman—with support and humor, she demanded I get closer, reaching through layers of memories to find precisely what happened and how it affected me and those I knew and loved.

And especially to Lenard Politte, Frank Rydzewski, Father Perez, and all those who served with me in the 95th Evacuation Hospital in Vietnam.

ABOUT THE AUTHOR

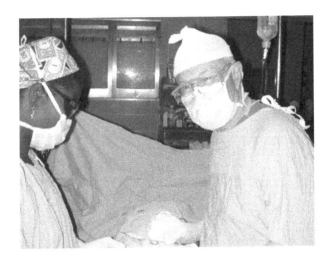

Dr. William Meffert first obtained a bachelor's degree from Duke University and then completed medical school and surgical residency at Yale University, including one year as the Winchester Fellow in Thoracic and Cardiovascular Surgery. After finishing his training, he volunteered for service in the army as a combat surgeon during the Vietnam War. He then spent a thirty-year career performing cardiovascular surgery in Iowa. After retirement, Meffert volunteered as a surgeon in Haiti, Russia, and China and was appointed a consulting professor at the Stanford University Department of Surgery. He also became a certified flight instructor and worked as a carpenter for Habitat for Humanity.

A longtime member of the Pegasus Physician Writers at Stanford University, Meffert has had stories and articles appear in *AOPA Pilot Magazine*, the Vietnam Center and Sam Johnson Vietnam Archive, *Evergreen Review*, *The MacGuffin*, *Helix Literary Magazine*, WebMD, Ars Medica, and *Pegasus Review*, among others. *There Were No Flowers: A Surgeon's Story of War, Family, and Love* is a nonfiction book about his experiences as a surgeon in war. For more information, please visit www.williammeffertmd.com.

Printed in the USA
CPSIA information can be obtained
at www.ICGtesting.com
LVHW091301050524
779401LV00008B/374